ABOUT THE AUTHOR
Cara Stillings Candal

Cara Stillings Candal is a Senior Fellow at Pioneer Institute. She has an extensive background in national and international education policy and teacher development, and she is the author/editor of numerous articles and several books about school university partnerships, charter schools, and other structural innovations in education. Candal holds a B.A. in English Literature from Indiana University at Bloomington, an M.A. in Social Science from the University of Chicago, and a Doctorate in Education Policy and Leadership from Boston University.

THE FIGHT FOR THE
BEST CHARTER PUBLIC SCHOOLS
IN THE NATION

By Cara Stillings Candal

PIONEER INSTITUTE
PUBLIC POLICY RESEARCH

Acknowledgments

THE AUTHOR AND PIONEER INSTITUTE WOULD like to thank Ken Ardon for his substantial contributions to this book. The chapters in this book are in part derived from papers that Dr. Candal has produced for Pioneer Institute in the past 10 years, some of them co-authored with Professor Ardon. Ken's research on charter school demographics, outcomes, and finance are an important foundation for many of the recommendations provided in the pages that follow. In the areas of school funding and charter school finance, Ken's ability to make an opaque formula more transparent provides a very important lesson for how policymakers should think about improving the Commonwealth's mechanisms for funding all schools.

We would also like to thank the countless people who have provided insight and opinions on many of the issues discussed in this book. Among them are policymakers, legislators, charter school teachers, leaders, and parents. Also among them are stakeholders who do not support charter public schools but are incredibly committed to school improvement in Massachusetts nonetheless. All have given their time: providing interviews, enabling observations of schools, and reading and providing feedback on this book and the many papers Pioneer has published on charter schools in the last decade.

We thank Julia Malakie and *The Lowell Sun* for permission to use the image that appears on the cover.

Finally, we would like to thank Chris Sinacola for his tireless attention to detail, valuable feedback, and great sense of humor.

MISSION

Pioneer Institute is an independent, non-partisan, privately funded research organization that seeks to improve the quality of life in Massachusetts through civic discourse and intellectually rigorous, data-driven public policy solutions based on free market principles, individual liberty and responsibility, and the ideal of effective, limited and accountable government.

BOARD OF DIRECTORS

PIONEER INSTITUTE
PUBLIC POLICY RESEARCH

Contents

Foreword

Thomas Birmingham
and William Weld

IN THE AFTERMATH OF AN ILL-CONCEIVED ballot campaign in which Massachusetts voters overwhelmingly rejected raising the cap on charter public schools, the political impulse is to assume that this particular debate has been settled. In the pages that follow, Dr. Cara Candal skillfully demonstrates why that would be a mistake.

The charter school landscape that currently exists in the Commonwealth is grounded in the 1993 Massachusetts Education Reform Act (MERA). This landmark legislation, which contained the most significant changes to the state's education system in generations, has been instrumental in making Massachusetts public schools the best in the nation. We were proud to have played central roles in the creation of this law in our former positions as Governor of Massachusetts and Senate Chairman of the Joint Education Committee. We would also like to acknowledge the significant contributions Mark Roosevelt, the then-House Chair of the Education Committee, made in the creation of this law.

Forces at both the national and state levels created the need for this legislation. In the early 1990s, lawsuits filed across the country were challenging inequities in state education financing systems. A notable 1990 New Jersey Supreme Court decision ordered the state to bring financing in poorer urban districts to equality with spending in wealthier ones.

Similarly troubling disparities existed in Massachusetts. To give one example, school districts in Wellesley were receiving approximately $25,000 per pupil, while students in Mattapan were receiving only $6,000.

As a result of the state's broken educational financing system, countless urban minorities were trapped in failing public schools. The misguided practice of social promotion was widespread, frequently causing students to graduate from high school without the basic skills or knowledge needed to succeed in college or the workplace. Parents desperately sought alternatives to these failing schools for their children, but few options existed.

In its 1993 ruling in *McDuffy v. Secretary of the Executive Office of Education,* the Massachusetts Supreme Judicial Court (SJC) challenged the Commonwealth's system of educational finance and standards. The SJC determined in *McDuffy* that the state, rather than individual localities, was ultimately responsible for ensuring that every child received a quality education, regardless of their economic status or the fiscal situation of the community in which they lived.

The MERA included a comprehensive set of measures for addressing these challenges. It established a new system for financing schools, known as the foundation budget, which ensured that each district had sufficient revenues to provide every student with an adequate education. The act set high standards that students would be required to meet and created a statewide assessment system called the Massachusetts Comprehensive Assessment System (MCAS) for measuring progress towards those goals. As Dr. Candal explains, the foundation budget and MCAS made Massachusetts one of the first states in the nation to link educational funding to standards and accountability for outcomes. This was the "grand bargain" that served as the foundation of the MERA.

To provide parents with more public education options for their children, the MERA also included a provision establishing 25 charter schools in the state. The cap on charter schools has since been raised on several occasions, most recently in 2010.

The latest attempt to raise the cap took place in 2016, when the legislature came up short in its effort to craft compromise legislation and then the electorate voted down a cap increase at the ballot box later that fall. Current Massachusetts Governor Charlie Baker was supportive of those efforts and continues to advocate for expanding charter schools in the Commonwealth.

Unfortunately, the conditions that led to the creation of charter schools in the MERA continue to persist. Although Massachusetts's public schools improved and became the nation's best in the wake of reform, not everyone has shared equally in the benefits.

The achievement gap between more affluent students and their less privileged peers remains. Today, the majority of students in the Commonwealth's urban districts attend schools whose performance ranks them in the bottom 20 percent of public schools statewide. Most of those children are poor, black or Latino, and many are immigrants.

Meanwhile, nothing has proven more effective at closing the achievement gap than our charter schools, which are the best-performing in the country. A Stanford University study found that Boston charters are doing more to close gaps than any other public schools in America. Statewide, charter schools dramatically outperform their district counterparts.

In recent years, Massachusetts charter schools have also been educating a growing percentage of English language learners and special needs students. Charters had long lacked the information required to reach out to these students, but a 2010 law mandated that district schools provide charters with the necessary contact information and required charter schools to submit plans for recruiting these students.

Today charter schools are on a path, within a few years, to enroll virtually the same percentage of English language learners and special needs students as the districts their students come from. A number of studies also show that these populations perform better in charters than in traditional public schools.

One of the reasons Massachusetts charter schools are so good is that the limited number of available charters has required that great care be taken to choose the very best from among numerous charter applications. Demand for the schools is high, as demonstrated by the tens of thousands of students on charter school waitlists, and we believe modest expansion would not compromise quality.

One way to help ensure charter school quality remains outstanding would be to eliminate the Commonwealth's so-called proven provider requirement. Currently, the percentage of possible charter seats doubles in school districts that rank in the bottom 10 percent statewide. But any seats above the original cap can only be offered by operators with a track record of success in Massachusetts. The result discourages innovation by the very element of education reform designed to inject innovative ideas into public education.

Charter schools' success has been achieved without sabotaging the school districts from which their students come. Unlike in other states that have charters, Massachusetts school districts are reimbursed for students who choose to transfer. Over six years, districts receive reimbursements equal to more than two years of funding for every student they lose to a charter school.

Massachusetts's Education Reform Act was fundamentally progressive legislation, providing far more state aid to poor school districts than to affluent ones. Unlike affluent students, their less privileged counterparts rarely have the option of attending a private school or moving to a community with better public schools.

In this volume, Dr. Candal takes a clear-eyed look at charter public schools in Massachusetts, describing their successes and noting areas in which they need to improve. Ultimately, she explains how we have waited decades for all school districts to deliver on the promise of providing all students with a first-rate education. Until they do, and as long as an option that does deliver on that promise exists, the charter school debate will rightly continue in Massachusetts. To settle for the status quo would be to compromise our students' potential for success.

ABOUT THE AUTHORS

Thomas Birmingham

Thomas Birmingham is the Distinguished Senior Fellow in Education at Pioneer Institute. He was previously the Executive Director of Citizen Schools Massachusetts and Senior Counsel with Edwards Wildman Palmer LLP. In 1991, Mr. Birmingham was elected to the Massachusetts State Senate, where he served as Co-Chairman of the Joint Committee on Education. He was one of the architects of the landmark 1993 Massachusetts Education Reform Act. Mr. Birmingham later served as Chairman of the Senate Committee on Ways and Means and Senate President. Mr. Birmingham graduated from Harvard College and Harvard Law School and is a Rhodes Scholar.

William Weld

William Weld is a Member and Principal at ML Strategies with Mintz Levin and the 68th Governor of Massachusetts. Before joining Mintz Levin and ML Strategies, Bill practiced law in the New York and Washington, D.C. offices of a large international law firm, where he established an extensive international consulting business in energy and natural resources. Bill was elected Governor of Massachusetts in 1990 and reelected in 1994 with 71 percent of the vote. During his term, he succeeded in reducing taxes while balancing the state budget, and his pro-business policies are widely considered to have made a positive impact on the state. Bill served as Assistant U.S. Attorney General in charge of the Criminal Division of the Justice Department in Washington, and as U.S. Attorney for Massachusetts, earning national recognition for his work fighting public corruption and white-collar crime. He also spent more than a dozen years practicing as a securities and anti-trust litigator. Additionally, Bill served as a staff member in both the U.S. House of Representatives, where he participated in the Watergate impeachment inquiry, and the U.S. Senate, where he worked for New York's Jacob Javits. Weld graduated with an A.B. *summa cum laude* from Harvard College, studied economics at University College, Oxford and graduated with a J.D. *cum laude* from Harvard Law School.

Introduction

Jim Stergios and Jamie Gass

IN THE DECADES FOLLOWING PASSAGE OF THE
Commonwealth's landmark 1993 Education Reform Act,
Massachusetts has become a recognized leader in K–12 public
education. While the Commonwealth can boast a number of
education policy achievements, no reform can measure up to the
success of its charter public schools.

During the first decade of education reform, Massachusetts
benefited greatly from a propitious and unique political climate.
Massachusetts's "ed reform" law was the handiwork of Repub-
lican Governor William Weld and two Democrats, Senator (and
later Senate President) Thomas Birmingham and State Repre-
sentative Mark Roosevelt. Rather than focusing on one specific
silver-bullet reform, it aimed to be comprehensive, with provisions that focused mainly on the establishment of charter public
schools, the development of academic standards and assessments, and equitable funding.

Weld's and especially Birmingham's roles were essential in
championing and stewarding implementation of the law through
the inevitable policy controversies. By 2005, the Commonwealth
became the highest-performing state in the country and in 2007
the sole American state to be internationally competitive in
public education.

The law aimed to provide charter public schools with
substantial autonomy in return for strict accountability for
outcomes. The schools could organize around a specific mission

and, to increase their likelihood of success, lawmakers gave them freedom to set school budgets, extend the school day and year, and select their own faculties and staffs.

The results have been remarkable. Numerous academic studies have found that Massachusetts charters dramatically outperform the districts from which their students come; a number of urban charter schools score first in the entire Commonwealth on various MCAS tests. Charter students also have higher SAT scores, participation rates in Advanced Placement (AP) classes, and percentages of students taking and passing AP tests.

Recent studies also show that Boston charter schools have low attrition rates compared to the city's district schools, and that charter school English language learners and students with special needs outperform their Boston Public Schools counterparts.

In addition to improving students' academic outcomes, lawmakers envisioned that the combination of autonomy and strict accountability for results would spark innovation. There too, Massachusetts charter schools have paid handsome returns.

Boston's Codman Academy Charter School is located next to a health center and integrates promotion of the physical health of its students, families and the surrounding community into its mission and curriculum. Phoenix Charter Academies serve vulnerable students such as those who have dropped out, are homeless, have no families, or have otherwise struggled in traditional schools.

In Central Massachusetts, the Francis W. Parker Charter Essential School focuses on promoting inquiry, expression and attentiveness. The school emphasizes the development of specific "habits of learning" and uses innovative portfolios to assess student growth over time.

At Match Charter Schools, each student's school day includes high-dosage individual and small group tutoring in key academically tested subjects. After the implementation of Match's tutoring program, student achievement, as measured by state English language arts tests, rose by the equivalent of a year's worth of additional instruction.

Given the importance of teacher quality, many Massachusetts charter schools invest heavily in teacher hiring and training. The Edward Brooke and Match charter networks have developed their own competitive teacher induction programs. At Match, many of those who enter the program began as tutors.

Even though charters generally can't match district salaries (more on that later), they recruit from a higher quality teacher pool than their district counterparts. *U.S. News & World Report* found in 2015 that 86 percent of teachers at Boston Collegiate Charter School graduated from "selective" or "highly selective" universities. A 2010 study found the number was about two thirds for the Boston Public Schools.

Investing in teachers doesn't end with the hiring and initial training processes. David Osborne of the Progressive Policy Institute has noted that principals, deans and senior teachers spend a great deal of time regularly observing and providing feedback to teachers.

Nothing about Massachusetts charter schools has been more controversial than the manner in which they are funded. But while optics and perception have been problematic, the Commonwealth has largely gotten the funding formula right.

The goal of any charter school funding formula should be to have the money follow the children from the districts from which charter students come. The Massachusetts formula does that to a great degree, adjusting for variables like grade level and low-income status.

Massachusetts goes a step further to aid district schools. In a move meant to ease the transition and account for fixed costs, it is the only state to reimburse districts for students choosing to attend charter schools. School districts receive full reimbursement the first year after a student leaves and a 25 percent reimbursement for each of the next five years.

Charters do face inequitable facilities funding. School districts have access to Massachusetts School Building Authority money, but charter schools do not. Instead, charters receive just an $893-per-student annual facilities payment, which comes out to far less than districts receive. This inequity helps explain why charters are generally unable to match school district teacher salaries.

So, Massachusetts public charter schools have a stellar track record for academic performance and innovation, even as they boast a funding formula that is more than fair to sending school districts. *Why then did Massachusetts voters overwhelmingly vote "no" when asked to raise the cap on charter schools in a 2016 state-wide ballot initiative?* It is an important question, for the ballot initiative was closely observed by charter school proponents and opponents nationwide. Initially, one can observe several contributing factors:

1. In Massachusetts, where charter public schools are highly urbanized, the ballot campaign to increase charter public schools was based on a (faulty) electoral theory that altruism toward other people's children will overcome powerful concentrated interests at the ballot box. It did not help that the ballot initiative was poorly written and the proponents' campaign ineptly run.

2. Numerous changes to state tests after the adoption of Common Core academic standards in English and math in 2010 made it difficult, if not impossible, to understand the performance of our public schools. It was especially hard for the public to understand just how badly urban schools are still doing in the Commonwealth. In addition, between 2010 and 2015, state education officials reduced the rigor of the 10th grade MCAS, likely as a political compromise to drive up graduation rates.

3. The Commonwealth's K–12 education funding formula is largely opaque, but two numbers are clearly visible. One is the amount that follows students moving from district to charter public schools. There is a corresponding reduction in the number of students the district is responsible for educating, the number is exclusive of generous state reimbursements, and studies show that the finances of all but a small number of more affluent districts are largely unaffected by charter schools. Still, the so-called charter school tuition allowed opponents to identify hundreds of millions of dollars that charters were "siphoning" from school districts.

The other is the amount of reimbursement that the state pays to school districts when a student opts out of the traditional system to attend a charter public school. That amount is subject to appropriation, and although in most years the line item was fully or almost fully funded, opponents were able to point to some in which budget crises caused them to be slashed.

4. Then there is the impact of the 2010 state legislation, which, in response to the Obama administration's Race to the Top program, was the last time the charter school cap was raised. That legislation doubled the number of students who could attend charter schools, but only in districts that performed in the bottom 10 percent statewide. In addition, the law requires any new charter schools in low-performing districts in which the cap rose to be operated by "proven providers" that were already operating successful schools in Massachusetts.

Taken together, these two provisions altered the charter school brand in Massachusetts. Rather than a diverse group of innovative schools, most new charters were replications of existing, albeit successful, urban charter models. These developments allowed opponents to isolate charter schools and paint them as a purely urban phenomenon consisting of "tough love" or "no-excuses" schools. Historically, Massachusetts charter schools did in fact serve fewer ELL and special needs students than their district counterparts. Charters said it was because they had no way to identify and recruit the students. A reform included in the 2010 law for the first time required districts to provide charters with district student contact information. Armed with that information, charters began recruiting significant numbers of ELL and special needs students. If current trends continue, charters will soon educate similar percentages of these students as their district counterparts.

Even when advancing positive change, the 2010 law brought new— and problematic — regulation to Massachusetts charters. Even as the law allowed charter schools access to potential students, it required that they develop and have approved by the state Department of Elementary and Secondary Education highly detailed student recruitment plans. If charter schools were designed to have autonomy in return for accountability for results, why not simply hold them responsible for increasing their ELL and special needs populations rather than requiring and insisting on approval of detailed recruitment and retention plans?

The fact is the 2010 law marked a whole new wave of state regulation on the Massachusetts charter sector; one that upended the original deal of autonomy for strict accountability. Which raises a fundamental question: If charter schools have so dramatically outperformed their district counterparts, why are we forcing them to be more like district schools rather than the other way around?

It is no accident that successful charter networks like Achievement First and Rocketship have not shown interest in Massachusetts. KIPP, perhaps the best known of all charter networks, has two Massachusetts schools and no known plans to apply for additional charters. The juxtaposition of schools that are the nation's best at closing the achievement gap and the massive political opposition to them in progressive Massachusetts serves as the backdrop to Dr. Cara Candal's book — and the story makes for great reading. Good policy requires good politics to succeed, and she describes ways in which the Commonwealth should act as a cautionary tale when it comes to perception and the politics that inevitably surround the charter issue. But Dr. Candal aims to do much more. She clearly presents lessons other states need to learn from Massachusetts when it comes to establishing successful schools.

Dr. Candal's story captures well the successes and failures of the quarter century-long history of Massachusetts's charter school experience; even more importantly, she points to what it might mean for the next 25 years.

ABOUT THE AUTHOR

Jim Stergios

Jim Stergios is Executive Director of Pioneer Institute, a Boston-based think tank founded in 1988. Prior to joining Pioneer, Jim was Chief of Staff and Undersecretary for Policy in the Commonwealth's Executive Office of Environmental Affairs, where he drove efforts on water policy, regulatory and permit reform, and urban revitalization. His prior experience includes founding and managing a business, teaching at the university level, and serving as headmaster at a preparatory school. Jim serves on the Board of Overseers at Boston University, where he earned a doctoral degree in Political Science.

Jim has been interviewed on the *BBC, Fox News Channel, MSNBC,* and has appeared regularly on local television and radio news broadcasts, including *WBZ, WHDH, WCVB, NECN, Fox 25, WGBH* TV and radio, *WBUR's* Radio Boston, WBZ's Nightside with Dan Rea, and *WRKO.* Jim's opinion pieces have appeared in *The Wall Street Journal, The Boston Globe, The Weekly Standard, The Washington Times, The Daily Caller,* and regional newspapers throughout New England. He has been quoted in hundreds of news outlets across the country, including in *The New York Times, The Economist,* and *The Washington Post,* and speaks at national policy conferences.

ABOUT THE AUTHOR

Jamie Gass

Jamie Gass is Pioneer Institute's Director of the Center for School Reform. At Pioneer, he has framed, commissioned, and managed over 100 research papers and numerous policy events on K–12 education reform topics, including several with Pulitzer Prize-winning historians. Jamie has more than two decades of experience in public administration and education reform at the state, municipal, and school district levels. Previously, he worked at the Massachusetts Office of Educational Quality and Accountability as Senior Policy Analyst-Technical Writer and in the state budget office under two Massachusetts governors. In the 1990s, Jamie worked for the Dean of the Boston University School of Education/Boston University Management Team in its historic partnership with the Chelsea Public Schools. He has appeared on various Boston media outlets, as well as talk radio shows throughout the country. He has been quoted in *Bloomberg/Businessweek*, *The Economist*, *Education Week*, and *The Boston Globe*, and his op-eds are regularly published in New England newspapers, as well as in *The Wall Street Journal*, *The Weekly Standard*, *The Hechinger Report*, *Breitbart News*, *The Daily Caller*, *The Federalist*, *Education Next*, and *City Journal*. He's won school reform awards in Massachusetts and Florida for his work on U.S. History/civic education, vocational-technical schools, and digital learning. Jamie speaks on academic standards, school choice options, and school accountability at events across the country.

CHAPTER 1

A Brief History of Charter Schooling in Massachusetts

M ASSACHUSETTS'S CHARTER SCHOOLS HAVE been called some of the best public schools — charter or district — in the nation. Researchers have taken a great interest in Boston's high-performing charter sector, especially because so many Boston charters close persistent achievement gaps.

When the Massachusetts Legislature included charter public schools as part of its landmark Education Reform Act of 1993, supporters believed they could be an important way to provide greater educational opportunity to poor and minority students. But they had little idea of how charter schools would look in practice and, more importantly, how the processes of establishing and overseeing them would work. At the time, only a handful of states had experimented with charter schools, and no one could tell who, if anyone, was getting it right.

Charter schools in Massachusetts exist on the basis of the fundamental bargain that founders and early supporters of the charter movement — Ted Kolderie, Ray Budde, and American Federation of Teachers' (AFT) president Albert Shanker — conceived. They are public schools of choice that enjoy greater autonomy than district schools. In exchange for that autonomy, charters are held to a higher standard of accountability.

The Massachusetts legislators who created charters never questioned the components of the bargain, but there was disagreement about how it would be upheld and enforced. There was also disagreement as to how much the Commonwealth should invest in an unproven education reform. Who would oversee charter schools? How much and what kind of autonomy would they have? How many would be allowed?

The answers to these questions would shape the charter school movement in Massachusetts for decades to come. But at the time, few people realized how important they would be. This is because charter schools were but one small part of the Education Reform Act's much larger education reform agenda.

Charter Schools: "One Small Part" of Education Reform

Although they would come to be the most controversial aspect of the 1993 Massachusetts Education Reform Act, when written into the law charters were just one small part of a sweeping effort to overhaul public education. The end of the 1980s was a tough economic time, and into the 1990s school budgets across the U.S. were feeling the strain. Education activists in the Commonwealth watched closely as lawsuits in other states forced change in the way schools were funded.

A case decided by Kentucky's Supreme Court in 1989, *Rose v. Council for Better Education*, declared that the state had a responsibility to provide all citizens with an adequate education. The court mandated that the state "take fiscal action" to ensure that citizens had access to an adequate education, no matter where they lived and no matter how much money local communities could raise for schools. Advocates for education reform in Massachusetts and other states took notice, and a wave of "adequacy lawsuits" were filed throughout the country in the 1990s.[1]

In 1990, *McDuffy v. Secretary of the Executive Office of Education* arrived at the Massachusetts Supreme Judicial Court

(SJC). At stake was a system of school finance in which local communities bore the majority of the financial burden for schools; a system that resulted, according to the plaintiffs, in vast disparities in educational opportunity that broke down along lines of income and race.

In *McDuffy*, the SJC found that Massachusetts school funding relied too heavily upon local property taxes, resulting in funding and quality inequities so egregious that they were unconstitutional. The SJC determined that it is the duty of the Commonwealth "to provide an education in the public schools for the children there enrolled, whether they be rich or poor, and without regard to the fiscal capacity of the community in which such children live."[2] The SJC went on to outline the "seven capabilities" that every child in the Commonwealth should have upon graduation.[3]

The SJC's decision meant that localities would no longer bear the majority burden of providing an acceptable education. Reform-minded legislators had been anticipating and preparing for the plaintiff's victory in *McDuffy*; MERA became law just three days after the SJC handed down its decision.[4]

The MERA provided a new system of financing schools, which included a "foundation budget." Each cycle, the Legislature determines the minimum level of per-pupil revenue school districts require to provide students with an adequate education. In cases where local communities cannot raise these minimum funds through the property tax, the Commonwealth is obliged to make up the difference. The amount the Commonwealth provides localities is referred to as Chapter 70 aid.[5]

But MERA wasn't only about closing revenue gaps. It also mandated the creation of state curriculum frameworks in core subject areas and a statewide assessment system to determine whether localities were successfully teaching those frameworks. The Massachusetts Comprehensive Assessment System was conceived as a "check" to ensure that government was getting a return on its investment.

The foundation budget and MCAS set precedent: Massachusetts was one of the first states to tie educational funding to

Massachusetts Education Reform Act, 1993

(1) **Access:** The state ensures that each child has an adequately funded education by establishing a foundation budget.

(2) **Outcomes:** The state determines what each child should know and be able to do upon graduation. The state establishes minimum competency standards and tests to hold schools accountable for helping students meet those standards.

(3) **Opportunity:** The state provides for diverse and innovative school models in the form of charter public schools.

standards and accountability for outcomes. Along with a few others, such as New York and Texas, it would eventually become a model for the George W. Bush administration's landmark reauthorization of the *Elementary and Secondary Education Act*, better known as *No Child Left Behind*.

In the larger context of Massachusetts education reform, a provision to establish 25 charter schools across the state garnered comparatively little attention. But the first 25 charters were the result of a quiet and consistent push from outside of the Commonwealth's education establishment to provide parents with more public education options.

Building a Charter School Law from the Outside In

When Education Reform passed in 1993, the term "charter school" was still relatively unknown. Ray Budde, a New York educator credited with coining the term, proposed in a 1988 book that "teams of teachers could be 'chartered' directly by a school board for a period of three-to-five years." In Budde's vision, "No one — not the superintendent or the principal or any central office supervisors — would stand between the school board and the teachers when it came to matters of instruction."[6]

Budde's proposal gained traction when AFT leader Albert Shanker endorsed it in *The New York Times* later that year, noting that change was needed but too often sidelined in district schools "for no good reason."[7] Minnesota became the first state to pass charter school legislation in 1991, about the same time that key Massachusetts legislators were starting to focus on reforming the Commonwealth's approach to school finance and accountability.[8] Key players such as Mark Roosevelt, House Chair of the Joint Committee on Education, his Senate counterpart Thomas Birmingham, Senate President William Bulger, and then-governor William Weld took notice of what was happening in Minnesota. They were especially interested, according to Birmingham, "in the promise that the charter concept held for disadvantaged students."[9]

At the same time, the charter idea was becoming popular in academic and business circles. In 1992, Pioneer Institute published a book by Stephen Wilson that envisioned turning Boston's schools around by giving them "increased autonomy in exchange for proof of better results."[10] After reading the book, State Street Bank President William Edgerly became a quiet champion for the charter concept in the Commonwealth.

For nearly 20 years Edgerly had invested time and money in the Boston Public Schools through a program known as the Boston Compact, which guaranteed jobs for graduates if the district could show incremental but steady progress. But he became disillusioned with the effort when it failed to effect real improvement. In a 1993 *Boston Globe* article, Edgerly critiqued the Compact, saying, "business lived up to its end of the bargain, the schools could not."[11]

As Edgerly tracked the establishment of charter schools in other states, he saw potential for the change he had hoped for under the Compact. He thought charters could be a "way for business and community leaders to impact the system from the outside in," something they hadn't been able to do in the past.[12]

Timeline of the Charter Movement

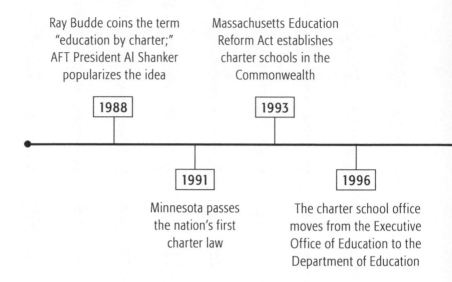

Ray Budde coins the term "education by charter;" AFT President Al Shanker popularizes the idea

1988

Massachusetts Education Reform Act establishes charter schools in the Commonwealth

1993

1991

Minnesota passes the nation's first charter law

1996

The charter school office moves from the Executive Office of Education to the Department of Education

Including charters in the MERA would require a coming together of the Senate and House. Senators William Bulger and Thomas Birmingham persuaded their colleagues that charter schools could be an important component of education reform. But the House questioned how the powerful state and local teachers' unions would perceive this new kind of school.

In the end, the only way the House would agree to pass a version of the MERA that included charter schools was to include in the legislation a cap on the number that could exist statewide: 25. Though such a conservative cap was unpopular with the Senate and the Weld administration, they saw it as a necessary trade-off to establish the charter movement in Massachusetts.

But the administration wasn't willing to compromise when it came to charter school authorizing. As states began to establish charter school laws in the 1990s, many adopted a model in which local school districts were responsible for establishing, overseeing, and holding charter schools accountable. The model is inherently problematic because charters are often painted

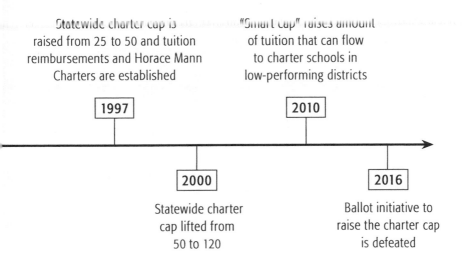

Statewide charter cap is raised from 25 to 50 and tuition reimbursements and Horace Mann Charters are established

"Smart cap" raises amount of tuition that can flow to charter schools in low-performing districts

1997

2010

2000

Statewide charter cap lifted from 50 to 120

2016

Ballot initiative to raise the charter cap is defeated

as competition for school districts; they give families another public school option.

Moreover, school districts have little incentive to grant charter schools the kinds of autonomy they require to succeed, such as the ability to extend the school day and year and offer innovative curricula and programming. Massachusetts school districts have traditionally sought to impose uniformity on their schools because uniformity, it is presumed, is bureaucratically efficient. Districts are also accustomed to bargaining with teachers' unions to establish lock-step pay grids and prescribed working days and years for all teachers. In the charter model, teachers in individual schools would have the *option* to unionize but most do not.

Instead of giving authorizing power to school districts, Massachusetts was purposeful in giving it to a single state entity, the Executive Office of Education (EOE), which the Weld administration had formed in 1991. The EOE operated independently of the Commonwealth's other education bureau-

The Charter School Bargain

AUTONOMY

ACCOUNTABILITY

cracy, then called the Massachusetts Department of Education (DOE), which was responsible for overseeing district schools.

Much like the charter school cap, the MERA's provision that charter schools be authorized by a single state entity has been a defining but sometimes controversial aspect of the Massachusetts approach to chartering schools. On the one hand, this model forecloses the possibility that school districts can authorize charter schools. This is important because research overwhelmingly demonstrates that when districts authorize charters, charters fail to sufficiently differentiate themselves from district schools and often fail to produce strong academic outcomes.[13] On the other hand, the single authorizer model also forecloses other entities, such as universities and not for profits, from authorizing charter schools — authorizing models that have been successful in other places.[14]

Another signature feature of the Commonwealth's charter school law is the funding formula, which is distinctive in two ways: First, it ensures that charter public schools receive the same per-pupil tuition rate (provided by the state) as their district counterparts.[15] The second distinctive aspect of the formula came later. It was devised in consideration of the financial strain that districts can experience when they lose students. Since 1997, the state has reimbursed districts for a period of time when they lose students to charter schools.

Both these aspects of the charter school funding formula set Massachusetts apart from other states. In many states, charter schools receive less per-pupil funding than their district counterparts. In most states, districts receive no additional funding or other financial assistance when students choose to attend a charter rather than a district school.[16]

But these distinctive aspects of the law do not ensure financial equality for charter and district schools. Charters receive only a small state stipend for capital and facilities expenses, which means they have to raise money to pay rent or buy a building. Compared to districts, which can rely upon local revenue and ample funding from a state program designed to support the establishment and maintenance of public (district) school buildings, charters are at a financial disadvantage.[17]

This unfair funding scheme has posed challenges but has not been a detriment to most charter schools, which have been very successful, both academically and in terms of financial viability and sustainability. Some contend that charters, which "do more with less,"[18] prove that district schools are not efficiently run.

Of course, there are other aspects of Massachusetts's charter law that have helped Commonwealth charters to do much more for kids. The original law ensured that charters would have real autonomy in exchange for real accountability. Faithfully implementing the spirit of that law would take careful consideration, and the early years of chartering in Massachusetts are evidence that some degree of experimentation was necessary to get it right. The charter school movement was born of a push from outside of the education establishment, and its advocates grew the movement, slowly but surely, from the ground up.

Building a Charter School Sector from the Ground Up

The post-MERA 1990s were a time of both promise and turmoil in Massachusetts's schools. The MERA promised school finance reform. It also promised that the state would hold schools accountable for outcomes, but schools and districts didn't know what accountability would look like. Fear of the then-unknown MCAS might have outweighed concerns about the nascent charter school movement, but the state's powerful teachers' unions were still keen to express their distaste for the new reform. They were especially unhappy with the prospect of non-unionized public schools and saw charters as a threat to maintaining and growing their membership.[19]

It was in this time of uncertainty and union opposition that the relatively new Executive Office of Education, headed by Weld appointee Piedad Robinson, had to decide how it would approach the charter school authorization process. This included setting parameters for soliciting and accepting charter school applications, understanding what would constitute a strong charter school application, and thinking through how EOE would hold schools accountable.

There were different opinions even within EOE about what authorizing approach to take. Some felt EOE should "let a thousand flowers bloom" by prioritizing applications and schools that were innovative and diverse in their approaches. Others wanted a narrower focus on academic outcomes, stressing the opportunities that new schools with rigorous academic programs could provide to poor and minority students, especially in the state's urban centers.

Potential charter founders were excited. In the first application year (1994), EOE received 48 applications to open charter schools.[20] The first round of applications represented a diverse range of ideas about pedagogical and curricular approaches. They also taught EOE staff about how to design a sound application process. It was clear from some of the applications that "applicants hadn't really considered some of the realities of running a school." EOE would "have to figure out what it wanted to see from applicants and in what kind of detail."[21]

The charter school cap would also play a large part in shaping the Massachusetts application and authorization process. In the first year after the MERA was passed, EOE approved 15 charter school applications, leaving room for only 10 more charters to open in subsequent years, unless some of the inaugural cohort failed to survive.[22] Thus it was soon after the advent of charter schooling in Massachusetts that EOE began to take a more risk-averse approach to authorizing.

In the mid-1990s EOE began to evaluate applications by asking three specific questions:

- Is this application espousing a philosophy and methodology that can raise student achievement?
- Will the school, as proposed, be financially viable?
- Do the applicants have the experience and skill it takes to run a school?

An approach to authorizing that values these questions, especially the first one, places an emphasis on high-quality educational opportunities and strong student achievement outcomes. Massachusetts's charter schools have been defined by this approach to authorizing from almost the beginning.

In part because of this approach, the Commonwealth's reputation for chartering excellent schools grew, even as authority for authorizing charter schools shifted. The Weld administration eliminated the EOE in an attempt to streamline government. In doing so, it also moved authority for charter school authorizing to the Board of Education (BOE). The charter school office, which would make important authorizing recommendations to the BOE, moved into what is now called the Department of Elementary and Secondary Education (DESE).[23]

Weld's move garnered criticism from charter advocates wary of overregulation. Whereas EOE operated independently of the larger state education bureaucracy, moving authorizing authority to the BOE, which would ultimately take most recommendations from DESE, meant the charter school office would be a part of the very bureaucracy it was created to circumvent. According to Ed Kirby, a member of the EOE's original charter school team, once authorizing responsibility fell to BOE and DESE, regulatory burden and the piling on of unnecessary bureaucratic processes began to undermine the original chartering ethos of the EOE, which greatly valued school autonomy.[24]

But the move was not immediately felt, and most charter advocates were more worried about the MERA's charter school cap than about a more regulated approach to authorizing. Lobbying to raise the charter cap of 25 had begun as soon as the first round of authorizing was completed in 1995. The lobby was spurred in part by the creation of a waiting list of approved charter schools — schools that the charter office deemed worthy of approval but that it wouldn't approve until there was more room under the cap.[25]

And there were other reasons to raise the cap. Massachusetts's first charters were getting noticed, even in international publications like *The Economist*, which lauded them for providing alternative schooling options to those who could benefit most from them.[26] More importantly, citizens were taking notice. By 1997, there were already 5,000 students on charter school waiting lists, vying for spots in 24 existing schools.[27]

This community demand for charters, especially in places like Boston, was hard to ignore. Parents felt that many charters were offering real alternatives for students. According to Karin Wall, a Boston charter school parent from 1998 on, "In the early days, those of us who took advantage of charters knew that they were offering something different: they were small, the academic programming was more rigorous, and they were safe places where motivated students could learn. In addition, as a parent, the schools felt small enough to wrap your arms around and get involved alongside other parents who wanted to contribute to the place where their children were spending six to eight hours a day. We felt we had a voice.[28]

But parents and community advocates who wanted more charter options were up against a very powerful anti-charter lobby, including the Massachusetts Teachers Association, superintendents, and local school committees. Charter advocates knew they would need to organize to dispel the arguments — some would say myths — that the anti-charter lobby was advancing. A group called Citizens United to Raise the Cap, led in part by Lawrence and Nancy Coolidge of the Mifflin Foundation, raised money to launch a public awareness campaign in support of the cap lift.

Citizens United to Raise the Cap had an uphill battle. Even in the early days of MCAS, many charter schools were showing surprisingly strong academic results, but charter detractors questioned the validity of those results by suggesting (as they do today) that charters were "creaming" the best students. They also sought to convince the public that charter schools harm districts by taking away funding and resources.

At the time, there were little empirical data available to confirm or deny these arguments. Today those data exist, and they refute both claims (see chapters 2 and 5). Regardless of the reality, the anti-charter lobby was successfully advancing powerfully negative notions about charter schools to the voting public.

When the Legislature did raise the statewide cap in 1997 (from 25 to 50 charter schools) it did so with conditions attached, in part to appease the anti-charter lobby. The first condition was a significant change in the school funding formula. The Legislature established the state reimbursement program for districts that exists today, though some aspects of it have been altered.

In 1997, that meant that when a student opted to attend a charter instead of a district school, the state would first deduct the per-pupil tuition the district would have received for that student and send it to the charter school. Once all charter school tuition deductions were made, the state would then consider any change in the amount of charter school tuition that the district would have to pay from one year to the next, and reimburse the district for any increase in that tuition.

In other words, if a district lost more pupils (and more tuition) to charters in 1998 than in 1997, the state would reimburse the district for 100 percent of that tuition increase. The reimbursements would continue for an additional two years, first at 60 percent of the tuition increase and then at 40 percent. The idea was that, year over year, districts would feel less financial strain when students left the system and would be able, over the course of several years, to adjust to smaller operating budgets and fewer students.

The second condition of the 1997 cap raise was that 13 of the additional 25 charter schools that would be allowed under the cap would be a new kind of charter school — Horace Mann (also known as "in-district") charter schools. Charter advocates viewed the addition of these types of schools as a concession because Horace Mann schools require the approval of a local school committee and teachers' union. While the schools would have more autonomy than other district schools (such as freedom to extend the school day and even some flexibility around hiring and dismissing teachers), they were still subject to many constraints, such as the constraint that all teachers remain members of the local collective bargaining body (union).

The final condition of the 1997 cap raise was another kind of charter school cap. The legislature increased the number of charter schools that could exist statewide but it also limited the amount of money that individual districts can spend on charter school tuition. In 1997, this district cap limited charter school tuition payments to no more than nine percent of net school spending.*

Another modest cap raise occurred in 2000. Then-commissioner David Driscoll supported the increase, citing not only the excellent outcomes charters were achieving but also the great demand for them in many communities. Charters were also showing district schools what was possible. Noted Driscoll, "they have strong curricula, longer days, long waiting lists, and great parental involvement. They're working."[29]

One reason the charter movement was flourishing, despite the cap, was the Commonwealth's approach to charter school closures. From the beginning, EOE and then BOE and (now) BESE[30] have never hesitated to close charter schools when they fail to perform. Once established, charter schools have to continually prove themselves through a charter renewal process that takes place every five years.[31]

Since the first charter schools were approved in 1995, the state has revoked five charters and failed to renew two. In the vast

* MERA, Chapter 70, Section 8.

The Purposes of Charter Schooling

(1) Stimulate the development of innovative programs within public education;

(2) Provide opportunities for innovative learning and assessments;

(3) Provide parents and students with greater options in choosing schools within and outside their school districts;

(4) Provide teachers with a vehicle for establishing schools with alternative, innovative methods of educational instruction and school structure and management;

(5) Encourage performance-based educational programs; and

(6) Hold teachers and school administrators accountable for students' educational outcomes.[32]

majority of cases, charters were revoked or not renewed because of financial mismanagement or because the schools have failed to perform academically, as measured by MCAS results.[33]

Despite the clear success of so many charter schools, it would be a decade before the movement saw another opportunity to expand. Opposition to charters, led by state and local teachers' unions, remained so strong that in 2004 the Legislature passed a moratorium on charter schools as part of the state budget. Though the moratorium was vetoed by then-governor Mitt Romney, it was clear that the political climate for expansion was difficult.

Shifting the Sector in 2010

The charter movement was largely stagnant until 2010, despite evidence that many Massachusetts charters, particularly in Boston, were among the best schools — charter, district, or private — in the country. With years of MCAS testing data and, thanks to *No Child Left Behind*,[34] similar (though not comparable) test score data from other states, researchers were beginning to understand which schools were closing achievement gaps. For the first time in U.S. history, parents were empowered to understand, because of test score data, how much value, if any, their local school was adding to the average child's education.

In 2009, the Obama administration leveraged these data about high-performing charter sectors in Massachusetts and elsewhere to incent states to create more charter schools. In its RttT initiative, the administration awarded competitive grants to states that demonstrated certain commitments to school reform, among them charter school expansion.

In Massachusetts, the Patrick administration — which had formerly been lukewarm toward charter schools — led the charge to raise the charter cap. The administration's proposal, which was developed with some cooperation from organizations traditionally opposed to charters, such as the MTA, proposed to lift the cap in communities that most needed and wanted charters: urban centers such as Boston.

The 2010 legislation that was written in response to RttT, known as the *Achievement Gap Act*, instituted a "smart cap." It lifted the cap on the amount of money individual districts can pay to charter school tuition, rather than the overall cap that limits the number of schools that can exist statewide.

In 1997, the amount of total school tuition that districts could pay to charters for taking on district students was limited to 9 percent of net school spending. The *Achievement Gap Act* raised tuition payments to 18 percent of net school spending in the lowest performing 10 percent of school districts in the Commonwealth. Additionally, the legislation required that BESE give priority status to "proven providers" who submit charter applications for schools that open under the smart cap. Proven providers are applicants with "a record of operating at least one school or similar program that demonstrates academic success and organizational viability..."[35]

The concentrated cap lift and proven provider clause included in the 2010 legislation have fundamentally changed the arc of the charter movement in Massachusetts. Although charter expansion had stalled by 2010, the momentum that the cap lift spurred was uneven because the smart cap dictated that many of the new charter seats would be replications of proven programs rather than new, innovative offerings.

Moreover, the smart cap framed charter schools as a tool for turning around struggling and failing districts, especially in urban centers. While it is true that demand for charter schools has historically been concentrated there, the explicit, statutory language that called upon charter schools to close achievement gaps in low-performing school communities further circumscribed the role of these schools in perception and practice. Charter schools were now a "brand," meant to serve certain types of students (low-income students of color) in certain communities (urban centers) using certain methods (a no excuses pedagogical approach). Not only would suburban and rural residents have little impetus to think of charter schooling as an option under this legislation, would-be charter operators had no incentive to move outside of urban centers or to propose anything other than the "tried and true."

The reputation of charter schools as both "for" a certain type of student and "serving" a specific purpose became very clear in November 2016, when Massachusetts voters went to the ballot box to decide whether to again raise the cap on charter schools in low-performing districts. Amid largely unsubstantiated claims by the Massachusetts Teachers Association that charters drain money from districts, charter proponents told suburban voters "if you like your public school, Question 2 won't affect you."[36]

Charter supporters understood that suburban voters could determine the fate of Question 2 for those most likely to use charter schools (urban parents), so they pushed the idea that charter schools exist mainly to fill a void where only low-performing schools exist.[37] But what charter supporters failed to realize was that urban parents, too, were becoming dissatisfied with the charter options available to them. As one parent says:

> As charter schools became a "movement" the schools failed to realize that kids have diverse needs and desires. Many schools developed a brand; short on relationships, high on discipline. Other parents I spoke to during the ballot initiative mentioned feeling like they and their children were being "managed" instead of engaged. The laser focus on high academics and college admissions seemed to lose sight of the need for other outlets that motivate struggling students to try harder, such as the arts or sports and music, where kids may find a measure of success. Additionally, living, learning and teaching in the urban environment brings with it other challenges, sometimes social/emotional, sometimes financial, etc. Failure to recognize these challenges and the impact they can have on learning doesn't make them go away.[38]

In other words, some would-be consumers of charters seemed to feel that charters were becoming more and more like districts. Across the Commonwealth, the answer to Question 2 was a resounding "no." One of the most controversial and most expensive ballot initiatives in Massachusetts history, Question 2 is reflective of the confounding history of charter schooling in the Commonwealth.

In 2017, Massachusetts charter schools were the highest performing in the nation. At the same time, the growth of the charter sector in Massachusetts is among the slowest. The success of the Commonwealth's charter schools is attributable to thoughtful and, in many ways, conservative legislation and to a likewise thoughtful and conservative approach to authorizing charter schools. However, this risk-averse conservatism has defined the charter movement in a way that might cause its demise. If charter schools, which were meant to be "laboratories of innovation," are circumscribed to one type and even one geographic area, it is unlikely that they will flourish either in number or in quality as they once did.

This history and the tension around and within the Massachusetts charter sector make it worthy of deep study. Massachusetts is a model for other states when it comes to charter authorizing and operation, and the following chapters will outline much of what the nation can learn from the Commonwealth. But the slow demise of the sector should also serve as a warning for states interested in expanding high-quality school options for parents. In a time when those options feel more and more necessary, Massachusetts charter opponents have convinced most of the voting public that charters should not be a major vehicle for school choice and educational excellence going forward.

CHAPTER 2

Supply and Demand:

Profiles of Charter Schools and Their Students

THE COMMONWEALTH BEGAN APPROVING charter school applications in 1994. That first application cycle, notes former Secretary of Education Michael Sentance, was arguably the most diverse that the state has known in terms of geography, proposed curricula, and pedagogical approach. In 1994, the Commonwealth approved 15 charter schools. Shortly after, charter schools were opening in places like Boston, Easthampton, and Devens.[1] Some were focused on serving urban students and closing achievement gaps. Others offered curricula focused on the arts and cooperative learning. This was innovation: access to different types of public schools that families did not previously have.

Soon after that first application cycle, several factors conspired to concentrate charter school growth in urban centers. For one, the population density of urban centers meant greater demand for new school options. Second, the reputation of some of the Commonwealth's urban public schools added to the allure of charter school options: in the early 1990s, Boston was known as a low-performing urban district with low graduation and negligible college-going rates.[2] Just north of the city, the Chelsea Public Schools were under state control due to poor academic performance and financial mismanagement.[3] Finally, urban centers were particularly attractive to many charter school founders, eager graduates of some of the area's elite universities looking to become "social entrepreneurs."[4] Education was an area ripe for change and charter schools provided an avenue for those who wanted to innovate.

As the charter school movement grew, it also narrowed. With fewer seats available under the cap each year, more and more charter schools were established in the places where parents most wanted them. At the time, some urban public schools were dangerous and very few were rigorous. Urban parents who once used low-tuition urban Catholic schools as an alternative to districts migrated to charters, causing a noticeable decrease in urban Catholic schools.[5] Some of the early charters were like Catholic schools; the most important similarities were that they were structured, safe, and academically rigorous.

If charters attracted parents who were dissatisfied with districts, they also attracted parents who were savvy enough to evaluate different school options — district, private, and charter. This is what researchers refer to as "selection bias," the idea that only the most motivated students and families enter charter lotteries. Selection bias might have accounted for many charter school applications in the beginning of the movement, but that wouldn't remain the case.

As individual charter schools grew in size, they also grew in reputation. The MERA requirement that all public schools be held accountable for outcomes as measured by MCAS shone a spotlight on both low- and high-performing schools. Over time, charter schools in the Commonwealth's urban centers emerged as some of the highest performers on MCAS. Parents no longer needed to be "in the know" to understand which schools were graduating students at high rates and sending them to college. They heard it from family members and neighbors. They watched on local TV as students who won a seat in a charter lottery rejoiced while those who didn't looked pained, even cried on the sidelines.

Parents seemed to like these schools because they "sweat the small stuff."[6] They offered safe, structured environments. They extended the school day and year. Some provided students, who often came to them behind in basic skills, one-to-one tutoring. Almost all were growing their own cadres of highly trained and effective teachers. In contrast to many district schools, these charters were academically rigorous, and made no excuse for the failure of adults to educate all children. In particular, they refused to accept poverty and the circumstances that accompany it as a reason for academic underperformance.[7]

But for all they were offering, these schools still failed to attract certain types of families and students. The students they served were disproportionately black and low-income. Few identified as having disabilities. Even fewer identified as English language learners.

There were various reasons for this demographic tilt. Some schools very specifically pitched their services to low-income, urban parents. In many of the Commonwealth's urban centers, those parents tended to be black. The greater success that charters had, the more black parents sought them. Other groups, such as non-English-speaking recent immigrants, were more likely to remain in district schools. Some charters were effective in targeting and reaching this group, but overall the concept of charter schooling had not taken hold in immigrant communities.

But charter demographics began to shift in 2010. *An Achievement Gap Act* framed charter schools as tools for turning around low-performing districts. By design, it further concentrated charter growth in low-income communities of color. It also explicitly included English language learners and students with other special educational needs in that frame.

The legislation includes requirements that charter schools develop detailed recruitment and retention plans that specifically describe how they will target these special populations of students. Proof that schools are executing these plans is also a requirement of the charter renewal process; both new and existing charters are held accountable for serving special populations.[8]

Prior to 2010, many charter schools explained their low numbers of English language learners and students with disabilities as related to inefficiencies inherent in the student recruitment process. Because district schools were not required to share student addresses with charters, most did not. Charter schools, especially middle and high schools, therefore relied upon word of mouth and "boots on the ground" community campaigns to make families aware of their offerings. These campaigns often resulted in charter parents effectively recruiting their own friends and family members to schools.

Charters also faced another issue: many weren't visible. Residents tend to know where their neighborhood public school is located, but they might not see a charter school or know they have access to it. Many charter schools, which add students one grade at a time, use temporary rented spaces to house students in their start-up years. A parent might walk past a strip mall or YMCA several times a day and never know that it houses a charter school that her child could attend.[9] This problem can be exacerbated when language barriers exist. Recent immigrants may not have the social capital to navigate even traditional school systems, let alone alternatives.

Of course, none of these reasons explain why charters would have low numbers of students with special educational needs. One of the reasons charter operators have traditionally given for low numbers of special education students is an unwillingness to place students on Individualized Education Plans (IEPs) unless parents asked for it and/or the IEP was clearly warranted. Charter school leaders and teachers explain that families who come to them from district schools sometimes hide the fact that their children are on IEPs, whether for fear of stigma or a belief that the IEP is not necessary. Since documentation about a student's prior experience has traditionally been slow to transfer from one district or school to another, school leaders and teachers might not suspect that students have IEPs.[10]

Furthermore, some charter schools — in particular those that identify as no-excuses schools, believe that students are often incorrectly given IEPs. Many students, they argue, do not have a special need that warrants an individualized program but are behind because they have not previously had access to high-quality educational options. Schools that make this argument are careful to differentiate between students who need specialized learning or behavioral supports and those who simply require exposure to content they should have learned earlier in school.[11]

Since the late 1960s, researchers have known that racial/ethnic minorities and low-income students are placed on IEPs at rates higher than their white, more affluent peers.[12] And studies find that, too often, low-income and minority students are identified as having a special need when they may not. This "disproportionality," as it is called in the research, has lasting effects; "misidentified students are likely to encounter limited access to a rigorous curriculum and diminished expectations."[13]

Even if charters were serving fewer students with special needs because districts were misidentifying those students, it would be difficult to explain how some charter schools served virtually no students with special educational needs at all. The 2010 law held charters accountable for serving special populations and, as a result, spurred dramatic changes in charter school demographics. By 2015, most charters across Massachusetts looked more like their district counterparts than ever before.

The Changing Face of Charters

An Achievement Gap Act put in place several requirements that changed the demographics of Massachusetts charter schools. First, charters began to directly recruit from a pool of all students eligible to attend school in sending districts; no longer did they have to rely solely on word of mouth or "boots on the ground" campaigns. Second, with incentives from the state to recruit and retain more diverse groups of students, some proven operators proposed programs designed specifically for special populations.

Match Charter Public school, for example, partnered with The Community Group, a charter operator in Lawrence, to open Match Community Day — a school based upon the proven Match model and designed with English language learners

Community Day Public Charter School - Prospect
Lawrence, MA

Community Day Public Charter School, Prospect was one of the first charter schools to open after the Legislature passed the Massachusetts Education Reform Act. It is located in Lawrence, Massachusetts and open to students from kindergarten to eighth grade. Community members, parents, and teachers founded the school, which has since expanded into a network of schools. It is operated by the not-for-profit Community Group, an organization that has been promoting high-quality education in Lawrence and beyond since its inception in the 1970s.

The demographics of Community Day have shifted as the population of Lawrence has changed, but the school has always had a reputation as a place where newcomers to Lawrence would be welcome and cared for. Students for whom English is not a first language apply to the Community Day lottery in disproportionate numbers. In 2017, 41 percent of students in the school were ELLs (compared to 31 percent of the Lawrence public school district). Students and families know the school is a welcoming place where all students have equal access to a high-quality education.

Community Day's philosophy of teaching English language learners (ELLs) is always evolving and always focused on meeting individual needs, but the school's leaders have cultivated tactics that work with students of all backgrounds. Providing students with language-enriched environments, no matter what subject they are studying, is one important tactic: "We don't just talk about math. We talk about how to talk about math," says Principal Mary Chance. Also critical to helping English language learners succeed is teacher development. Community Day seeks teachers who know the community and know the cultural backgrounds of Community Day students. School leaders use their charter school autonomy to hire without constraint and find the right talent. The school also consistently provides targeted, structured, development opportunities for teachers so that they may constantly refine their practices, both as individual practitioners and teams.

Phoenix Charter Academies Network

Phoenix Academies have an explicit mission to serve the Commonwealth's most disconnected youth — the chronically truant, court- and/or gang-involved students, those with special needs, English language learners, and young men and women who have already dropped out. The model is one of high standards, high expectations, and academic rigor coupled with "relentless supports" that help students who are alienated from school reconnect to their education. Across its three campuses in Chelsea, Lawrence, and Springfield, MA, Phoenix enrolls high numbers of students with special educational needs, the vast majority of whom have been underserved by schools they attended in the past.

The Phoenix philosophy of relentless support pervades everything the adults on the network's campuses do. It is a system undergirded by structures that facilitate student success. It is also a mindset — a way of thinking about and engaging with students — that turns traditional educational approaches on their heads. Through relentless support, Phoenix gives students every chance to meet their teachers' high academic expectations. Teachers never lower their expectations for an individual's success, they simply find every opportunity to help individuals succeed, no matter how long it takes.

Students can enroll in Phoenix quarterly, up to five times a year, allowing the school to capture more students before they choose to drop out of high school altogether. The quarter system also allows those already enrolled to "reset" when they have missed too much school or need an additional chance to master coursework. Phoenix forgoes traditional grade levels, opting instead to classify students as "Category I, II, or III." A student's category does not reflect his or her age (many of Phoenix's students have "aged out" of traditional schools). Instead, categories reflect the content students have mastered. "Mastery" does not equate with "seat time" at Phoenix. A student graduates when he or she has mastered the material, based on state standards, needed to graduate from high school and succeed in college.

The Phoenix model holds promise for at-risk students who have the potential to step back from the verge of dropping out of high school and go to college. But this isn't the only aspect of the model that policymakers, school administrators, and teachers should consider. What Phoenix has been able to help students do raises a question: Could more districts benefit from a Phoenix school or something like it, or should schools and districts look to Phoenix to learn to implement the best practices that it employs?

in mind. Excel Academies, which had always attracted large numbers of English language learners to its East Boston campus, opened a new campus in Chelsea, a city that borders Boston and also has high numbers of ELLs. Phoenix Academies, first opened in Chelsea in 2006, partnered with the district of Lawrence in 2012 to open a school for at-risk youth that deployed the Phoenix approach in a district setting. Lawrence, like Chelsea and East Boston, serves high numbers of ELLs. These collaborations and others were designed to expand successful charter school models to more students and more diverse groups of students.[14]

At the same time, schools that were doing more to make their offerings more attractive to special populations were seeing their recruitment efforts pay off. As soon as 2011, just a year after the new law, ELLs and students with other special educational needs applied to charter school lotteries in greater numbers. When City on a Hill Charter Public Schools, one of the oldest charter schools in the Commonwealth, opened its campus in New Bedford in 2014, 30 percent of students enrolled were students with disabilities. The same year, 19 percent of students enrolled at New Bedford High School were students with disabilities.[15]

By 2013, the percentage of ELL students enrolled in charter schools exceeded statewide averages of overall ELL enrollment. Even in communities like Boston, which has traditionally served large numbers of ELL students, ELL enrollment in charters more than doubled in five years and has continued to trend steadily upward.[16]

The same holds true for students with disabilities. By 2016, charter schools in Boston were serving students with disabilities at almost the same rate as the district.[17]

These demographic shifts are even more powerful in context: Charter schools admit students via lottery and only hold lotteries in certain grades. This means that some have more "stable" student populations than their district counterparts, which see larger numbers of students moving in and out of each grade level every year.[18] The rather dramatic increase in the numbers of students with special needs enrolled in charters since

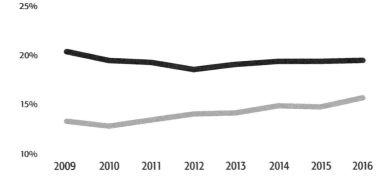

% Students with Disabilities in Boston Public and Boston Charters 2009-16

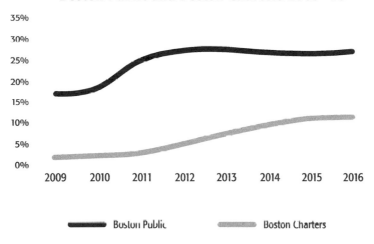

% English Language Learners in Boston Public and Boston Charters 2009-16

Boston Public ▬▬▬   Boston Charters ▬▬▬

2010 means that much larger numbers of students began to seek a charter school education after that time. Especially considering that not all students who apply to a blind lottery are admitted, charter schools would have had to see a rather large increase in demand for their services among these populations for the actual number of students enrolled to grow as it did.[19]

Evidence from one randomized control trial (a gold-standard in education research) conducted in 2015 supports this. The study found more students with disabilities applying to charter school lotteries after 2010 and a corresponding decrease in the number of students with disabilities enrolling in district schools in charter school entry grade years.[20]

Serving All Students:
Why Charter Demographics Matter

Why does the changing face of Massachusetts charter schools matter? Because as charter schools have recruited and retained a more diverse student population, they have become more accessible and equitable. If any public school, charter or district, offers a curriculum or pedagogical approach that parents want, parents should have access to that school. Some families and students will be highly motivated to choose certain types of schools, and others will have the knowledge and tools—the social capital—to navigate a sometimes confusing public school landscape. While we should never criticize parents for being motivated, it is problematic if any type of public school engages in practices that exclude categories of students or families.

From the earliest days of the charter movement in Massachusetts, charter schools have been accused of "creaming," and "selective push out." These phrases suggest that charters purposefully attract a certain type of highly motivated individual and that they actively discourage "unmotivated" individuals from using their services, even after they are enrolled.

In 2009, the MTA attempted to support these claims in a paper titled "Charter School Success? Or Selective Out Migration of Low-Achievers? Effects of Enrollment Management on Student Achievement."[21] According to the MTA, not only were charters failing to serve ELLs and students with disabilities at rates similar to their district counterparts, they were also pushing less able students out of their programs.[22] "Creaming" and "push out," said the MTA, were the reasons that charter schools were so successful on MCAS.

Although the MTA report provided no empirical evidence for its claims, until 2010, few charter operators could say that they were serving ELLs and students with disabilities at parity with districts. Furthermore, to refute claims of "push out," charters had little to offer but anecdotal evidence. While the large increases in ELLs and students with disabilities post 2010

ATTRITION

The **Attrition Rate** represents the percentage of students who were enrolled at the end of one school year and did not remain in the same school in the following fall.

WEIGHTED ATTRITION

It is not always useful to compare attrition rates between public school districts and charter schools in Massachusetts (which are classified as their own districts) because students can move among schools in districts and not be counted as leaving. At a charter school, every student who leaves at the end of the year factors into its attrition rate, no matter where students go. Massachusetts therefore uses a "weighted attrition rate" to make comparisons between districts and charters, averaging attrition rates across all schools in a district and then weighting that average by the number of students enrolled in each school.

refute the MTA argument, it would ultimately be more complicated to prove that charter schools weren't counseling less able students to leave. In 2009 and even today, some charter schools have much higher than desirable attrition rates, which is the rate at which students leave one school for another between academic years.[23] High attrition rates could suggest that students were being encouraged to leave charters.

But attrition is complicated, and it can be difficult to know *why* students leave schools from one year to the next. Some might be dissatisfied with a school's program. Other students might move away. The bottom line is that neither charter opponents nor proponents, let alone policymakers, could really know if claims of charter "push out" were true until the Massachusetts Department of Elementary and Secondary Education began collecting and publishing attrition data for all schools, which it did post 2010.

Soon after, it became clear that, on the whole, the most successful charter schools were not achieving their results because they were pushing students out. On the contrary, many of these schools were doing a better job of keeping students enrolled than their district counterparts. By 2014, charter proponents could confidently say that weighted attrition rates for Boston charter schools, some of the most academically successful schools in the country, were lower than the weighted attrition rates of Boston's district schools. The same held true for successful charter schools in the Commonwealth's "gateway cities," like Lawrence, where all schools, charter and district, are more likely to serve high numbers of ELL students.[24]

More important than the revelation that academically successful charter schools are not pushing students out, is that the same schools have continued to achieve superior academic outcomes even as their student demographics have shifted. ELLs and students with disabilities are often called "special populations" because schools support them differently than students who are English speaking and/or don't have significant learning or behavioral challenges.

Several studies conducted from 2009 on confirm that ELLs and students with disabilities enrolled in charter schools achieve higher MCAS scores than their district counterparts.[25] One 2015 study is of special note because it used a randomized control trial approach. It evaluated the performance of English language learners and students with disabilities who applied to charter school lotteries and were admitted, to those same types of students who applied to charter school lotteries but were not admitted. Using this approach, Elizabeth Setren of MIT was able to confirm that the superior performance of ELLs and students with disabilities enrolled in Boston's charter schools was not due to selection bias—in other words, there was no evidence that the ELLs and students with disabilities enrolled in charters were somehow differently motivated than their district school peers.[26]

The results of Setren's studies and others, to be discussed in greater detail in chapter 3, point to the very high quality of education that most Massachusetts charters, particularly in Boston, have. Understanding what makes these schools work has been the topic of countless articles and several books. While all successful schools have many things in common, the main feature that Massachusetts's high-performing charter schools share is that they exist in a policy environment that sets a high bar for success.

As the charter movement has matured, the criteria for what defines a successful school have changed. Whereas test scores used to be the main measure, DESE and BESE now consider other factors related to access and equity—such as demographics, attrition, and even school suspension rates—in evaluations of charter school quality. Looking more closely at these factors has held charter schools to account for implementing high-quality programs that will serve all students. Because charter schools have, by and large, responded to this type of accountability by continuing to produce positive outcomes, they have been able to refute claims of "creaming" and selective "push out."

Of course, as BESE, the Commonwealth's only authorizer, considers which outcomes are the best measures of charter school success, it must also consider how to measure those outcomes in a manner that doesn't overburden charter schools with regulations or subvert their autonomy. Regulations that simply force charter schools to comply by writing a recruitment and retention plan for special populations are meaningless if BESE is not examining the outcomes of those plans. Worse, forcing charters to go through the motions of producing paperwork threatens to take valuable time and personnel away from the business of teaching and learning. Many large urban districts face this problem — a problem that the charter school bargain of enhanced autonomy for strict accountability was meant to circumvent.

CHAPTER 3

Outcomes:

Measuring the Success of Massachusetts Charter Schools

W HEN THE LEGISLATURE INCLUDED CHARTER
schools in the Massachusetts Education Reform Act, it
cited six purposes. Charter schools were supposed to:

1. stimulate the development of innovative programs within public education;
2. provide opportunities for innovative learning and assessments;
3. provide parents and students with greater options in choosing schools within and outside their school districts;
4. provide teachers with a vehicle for establishing schools with alternative, innovative methods of educational instruction and school structure and management;
5. encourage performance-based educational programs; and
6. hold teachers and school administrators accountable for students' educational outcomes.[1]

Enhanced parent choice and innovation are the first things the MERA mentions in relation to charter schools, but policymakers and the public have focused much more on accountability, educational outcomes, and the performance-based educational programs that charters offer. There are various reasons for this.

Innovation and distinctiveness are highly subjective, and neither is easy to measure. Is a school that relies upon "traditional pedagogical approaches" innovative and distinctive if it exists in a market of "progressive" schools? Is a school that closes achievement gaps where others don't a distinctive school?

Standardized tests might be unpopular, but they are a comparatively reliable way to measure educational outcomes — they provide data about what students do and do not know. In the Education Reform/*No Child Left Behind* era, when most Massachusetts charter schools were growing, test scores became the primary way to measure school success.

Many successful charters have helped students perform well academically because they embrace standardized testing and focus relentlessly on outcomes. Terms such as "data-driven instruction," which describes how teachers use assessment and other data to inform decisions about student learning, are a best practice adopted out of the charter movement. Educators like Doug Lemov, a founder of Boston's Academy of the Pacific Rim Charter School, have become nationally known for helping schools across the country implement practices that dramatically boost student achievement.[2]

In the late 1990s, as MCAS was being developed and rolled out, there was a hint that charters — particularly those that adopted a no-excuses[3] approach — were helping students achieve outcomes that surpassed students in district schools. These results were particularly impressive because of the population these schools were serving — students who were disproportionately black and low income. According to conventional thinking at the time, these students weren't achieving in most school settings because they were trapped in a "cycle of poverty."

In 1996, DESE published a report citing the early successes of many charter schools, such as SABIS International Charter School in Springfield, whose students had shown a year and a half of growth in reading and math in just one year's time.[4]

Another DESE study, conducted during the 1999–2000 school year, found "64 percent of charter school students making greater than average gains in reading scores and 63 percent making greater than average gains in overall scores."[5] These early studies couldn't use MCAS, as it was still too young and unreliable. Instead, they analyzed student scores on norm-referenced tests, such as the Stanford 9 and Iowa Test of Basic Skills. Study results turned the attention of the nation on Massachusetts's charters; media outlets like *The New York Times* wrote about how these schools were closing what were once thought to be intractable achievement gaps.[6]

> The federal *No Child Left Behind Act*, which became law in 2001, required states to develop standards in core subject areas and tests to measure whether students were mastering standards. A precursor to NCLB, MCAS served as a model for other states as they designed their own standards and tests. Massachusetts Senator Edward M. Kennedy was one of the architects of *NCLB* and a great supporter of Massachusetts Education Reform.

But it would be MCAS, which has come to be known as one of the most rigorous criterion-referenced tests in the country, which would ultimately shine light on how consistently well charters were doing. Two studies conducted in 2006 and 2009, one by DESE and the other by the Boston Foundation, drew the same important conclusions: 1. charter schools were, as a group, outperforming district schools on MCAS, and 2. charter schools were meeting the needs of low-income, minority students particularly well.

The 2009 study is notable because it represents one of the first "gold standard" studies conducted of charter schools in the Commonwealth or anywhere else. Studies of school performance can be particularly difficult to quantify, in part because it is considered unethical for researchers to give one group of students a treatment and withhold that treatment from another. This approach, which is referred to as a randomized control trial (RCT), predominates in medical research, and helps investigators to understand whether the effects of a drug come from the drug itself or from something else.

Charter schools provide an unusual opportunity for researchers to conduct randomized control trials because families and students are not assigned to charters; they choose to attend. When families choose a charter but the school is oversubscribed, the school must admit students via a lottery because, by law, charters cannot discriminate as to whom they accept. There are, therefore, usually two groups of students associated with charter schools: those who applied to a charter school lottery and won a seat, and those who applied to a lottery but did not gain entrance. These charter lottery "winners and losers" are considered to be similarly motivated. That is, there is no reason to believe that students in one group are more capable or driven to succeed than students in the other. The lottery therefore provides researchers with a built-in control group.

In the 2009 study of Boston's charter, district, and pilot schools,[7] researchers from Duke, MIT, Harvard, and the University of Michigan used an RCT approach and found that "Boston's charters raise student achievement .09 to .17 standard deviations in English language arts and .18 to .54 standard deviations in math." The researchers also found the "estimated impact on math achievement for charter middle schools to be extraordinarily large." The middle schools studied "increased student performance by .5 standard deviations, the same as moving from the 50th to 69th percentile in student performance. This is roughly half the size of the black-white achievement gap."[8]

This study came at the same time as similar studies in New York and Chicago that also showed advantages for charter schools. But Massachusetts has continued to be an attractive place for charter research because its single authorizer model, comparatively rigorous high school exit examination, and sophisticated and transparent data collection make it easy for researchers to access the data they need to conduct RCT studies.

So, in the first decade of its existence, it was becoming clear that the Massachusetts charter experiment was working. Charter detractors, however, would try to emphasize unfair advantages charters might have to explain strong academic outcomes. The most common explanation, mentioned briefly in chapter 2, has been that charters "cream" only the most motivated students and "push out" others, including students with disabilities and English language learners.

As described in chapter 2, two studies, one conducted by Elizabeth Setren of MIT in 2015, and DESE's 2016 Charter School Demographic Report, find that charter school attrition (the rate at which students leave a school from one year to the next) is the same or lower than that of district schools. This invalidates the argument that charter schools, as a group, push students out. More importantly, however, the Setren report finds that charters help students with a diverse range of special needs perform very well academically. The study finds that "charter school attendance [in Boston] has large positive effects for math and English state exam scores for special needs students... one year of charter attendance for a special needs student narrows the special needs achievement gap."

These findings suggest that Boston's charters are doing something previously unheard of — closing achievement gaps with diverse types of students. Setren's study and others have helped these schools to earn a reputation as models for education reform.

But few studies have brought the Commonwealth as much attention and acclaim as a series of studies published by the Center for Research on Education Outcomes at Stanford University (CREDO). These studies have, over the years, suggested that Massachusetts's charters are among the best schools — district, charter, or private — in the country.

While CREDO's national charter school studies have been criticized for not using a gold standard RCT approach, its studies of urban charter schools, which look more specifically at the cities and regions with the greatest concentrations of charters, draw conclusions similar to some of the highest quality RCT research. When it studied Boston's charter schools, CREDO's findings were impressive: Its 2013 study concluded that Boston charter school students outperformed their district school peers by more than .34 standard deviations in reading and .36 standard deviations in math. "This translates to an additional 12 months of learning in reading and 13 months in math each school year, as compared to students in the district schools close to each charter region studied."[9]

CREDO's statement is even more impressive considering that the Commonwealth of Massachusetts has repeatedly been cited as one of the highest performing education systems in the country. This includes urban districts, like the Boston Public Schools, which have improved dramatically in the past 20 years.

But standardized test outcomes aren't the only way to measure school effectiveness. In fact, as states and localities shift from a test-based accountability mentality molded in the *No Child Left Behind* era and begin to focus, in the era of the *Every Student Succeeds Act,* on different and additional outcomes for the purposes of holding schools accountable, charters in Massachusetts and beyond will likewise focus on other measures of student success. Among them are graduation, college-going, and college-persistence rates. Indicators of college preparation, such as AP exam taking and results, are also increasingly important.

Translating Test Scores to College Preparation and Persistence

Standardized tests are important accountability tools. In the context of the MERA, they've helped policymakers understand which schools are equipping students with basic skills and which are closing achievement gaps. But standardized tests don't predict post-secondary success. A school could help students achieve strong outcomes on standardized tests, but most criterion-referenced tests are designed to indicate minimum competency in a given subject, not whether a student is prepared to succeed in college.

Over time, Massachusetts has come to realize this. It has also remained committed to preparing students for college, whether or not they ultimately choose to go. As a result, schools are accountable for multiple measures of academic achievement. Some, like standardized tests, are designed to capture basic data about competence, access, and equity. Others are better indicators of college preparedness.

One basic measure of whether a high school is serving students well is the dropout rate. If students leave high school before graduation, they are unlikely to be captured by test results, so understanding how many students schools start with and how many complete high school may be even more important than test scores for purposes of accountability, equity, and access.

The Commonwealth calculates the dropout rate by determining the percentage of students in a "class" (beginning at grade 9) who do not attend school the following year and did not transfer to another school. While this is an imperfect calculation in that students and families don't always report when they move out of a district, the state, or even the country, looking at dropouts from a "class" or cohort perspective (as opposed to counting, for example, only students who make it to grade 11 or 12) is a rigorous way to assess student dropout; not all states are inclined to subject schools to such rigorous measures.[10]

Statewide, the dropout rate has declined in recent years and is low compared to other states: in 2015–16 only 1.9 percent of students dropped out of high school.[11] That number rises when researchers look only at students who are economically disadvantaged. This sub-group of students, which is at greater risk of dropping out due to factors associated with living in poverty, dropped out of high school at a rate of 4.1 percent in 2015–16.

Boston has the greatest concentration of charter schools in Massachusetts and therefore provides a window into how charters, in general, fare when it comes to retaining students and helping them graduate. Dropout rates in Boston's charter schools, after controlling for charters that cater specifically to students at risk of dropping out, were less than 1 percent in 2016–17. In the sending district, Boston Public Schools, the dropout rate for the same year was 4.7 percent.

And the lower dropout rates in Boston charter schools lead to higher graduation rates. The four-year graduation rate for Boston's charters was roughly nine to fifteen percentage points higher than Boston Public Schools for a decade, although the gap narrowed substantially in 2016.[12] The five-year graduation rate at Boston's charter schools is even higher, as is the gap between charter schools and Boston Public Schools. In 2015, more than 93 percent of Boston's charter school students graduated in five years, compared to only 76 percent in the Boston Public Schools.

The five-year graduation rate is more than an indicator of whether schools are successfully graduating students. In some cases it is an indicator of *how* schools are preparing students for life after high school.

The vast majority of urban middle school and high school charter operators suggest that when students arrive at their schools they are often several grade levels behind in core subject areas. Many charters have become well known for closing overall achievement gaps by focusing relentlessly on filling the knowledge gaps students have when they enter school and then doing the additional work of making those students college ready. When studies of charter school achievement note that schools are providing students with more than one or even several years of learning in one year or less, they are recognizing the work that schools do to "catch students up" to grade level in short periods of time.

Research finds a correlation between being held back, or prevented from graduating with one's cohort, and dropping out of school.[13] This is one reason why some schools engage in "social promotion," promoting students from one grade level to the next to keep them with their cohort, even if they haven't mastered the relevant content. Social promotion too often results in students leaving school without academic and life skills. Many Boston charters have stated explicit opposition to social promotion,[14] opting instead to work with students for as long as it takes to get them ready for college.

Research also finds a correlation between high suspension rates and dropout and, on the basis of this research, Massachusetts tracks suspension rates at each school. High suspension rates have also come to be associated with the no-excuses pedagogy on which many successful charter schools first built their programs. While schools of all types work to replace out-of-school suspension, in particular, with other disciplinary tools, it is notable that in some of the state's most successful schools, charters included, attrition and dropout rates can remain low, even when suspension rates seem disproportionately high. A student's willingness to stay in a school despite tough approaches to discipline may be an indicator of the quality of education and breadth of opportunities the school provides.

Evidence suggests that when students stay in a Boston charter in particular, whether it is for four years or more, they are exposed to more curricular content and more opportunities that prepare them for college. In a 2016[15] study, Angrist et al. looked at the impact of Boston charters beyond standardized test scores. They found that the higher test scores these schools produce also predict gains in other areas, such as AP test taking, SAT scores, and even the types of colleges students attend:

Our findings suggest that the gains from Boston's high-performing charter high schools extend well beyond high-stakes tests. Charter attendance doubles the likelihood that a student sits for an Advanced Placement exam, with especially large gains in the share of students taking science exams. Attending a charter school quadruples the likelihood of taking an AP Calculus exam and increases the fraction of students earning an AP Calculus score high enough to qualify for college credit from 2%, for non-charter attendees, to 13 percent, for charter attendees. Charters also boost SAT scores sharply, especially in math. Importantly, our estimated SAT gains are about as large as the estimated gains on the state's high-stakes high school exit exam, in spite of the fact that SAT scores are unrelated to state-mandated accountability standards. Although overall college enrollment effects are not statistically significant, charter attendance induces a clear shift from 2-year to 4-year colleges, with gains most pronounced at 4-year public institutions in Massachusetts.

This study suggests that much more than "teaching to the test" is happening in Massachusetts's charter schools. In particular, the rates at which charter students in Boston and beyond are taking AP tests helps these schools provide opportunities to poor and minority students that didn't previously exist.

The opportunity gap in AP access has long mirrored the gap that poor and minority students experience more generally. As recently as 2003, only 11 percent of AP test takers were low-income, and fewer were minorities. Although the number of "low income graduates" with access to AP quadrupled between 2003 and 2013, access to AP for black students in particular has remained low. Access for Hispanic students is only slightly better.[16]

In the last decade, Massachusetts has made AP access for all students a policy priority, and the state has seen gains both in the number of students taking AP examinations and the number of students passing them. In 2005, 9.5 percent of the Commonwealth's black high school graduates "took at least one AP exam; in 2015, 35.2 percent did." And access has boosted outcomes. "In 2005, 3.4 percent of black high school graduates scored at least 3 on one or more AP exams; in 2015, 13.5 percent did."[17]

Charter schools have greatly contributed to the growing numbers of students taking and passing AP courses. While AP test taking has risen overall in Boston and other urban centers, it has remained even higher in the charter sector.

More importantly, AP access, test-taking, and test-passing rates remain high across the charter sector but uneven in some district settings. The City of Boston provides an excellent case study because of its demographic make up and concentration of charter schools. While AP test-taking has increased in BPS post 2010, the uptick has taken place mostly in the city's competitive exam schools. These schools admit students based on standardized test scores, unlike other city schools and Boston's charters. They are disproportionately white and higher income compared to their non-selective district counterparts.

When these selective schools are removed from AP data, an AP access and equity issue comes to light. In 2013, for example, 40 percent of black upperclassmen and 42 percent of Latino upperclassmen in Boston's charter schools took one or more AP exams. Those numbers drop to 16 percent and 22 percent, respectively, in Boston's non-exam district schools.

And AP passing rates are even more revealing: In 2015, 35 percent of Boston charter school students passed the AP test that they took, while 18 percent of Boston's non-exam school students passed their AP tests. These data suggest that Boston's charter schools are doing a much better job than their non-exam district counterparts of helping poor and minority students access and pass AP tests, which can aid in college entry and persistence. In fact, Boston's charters help their students pass AP exams at rates closer to their exam school — as opposed to non-exam school — counterparts.

Higher AP participation and passing rates could be one reason why charter schools have a reputation for high college acceptance and attendance rates, but they are only one of many supports schools provide to help students get into college. Charter schools and networks across the country, Massachusetts included, boast very high rates of college acceptance — in many cases as high as 95 to 100 percent.[18] These acceptance rates stand in stark contrast to those in most traditional school districts. Nationwide, less than 70 percent of high school graduates attend college immediately following high school.[19] Even fewer persist and graduate.

Advanced Placement by Sub-groups, 2016[20]

	Black		Hispanic		Economically Disadvantaged	
	Exams	Pass Rate	Exams	Pass Rate	Exams	Pass Rate
BPS Exam Schools	567	45.9%	492	52.8%	817	57.8%
BPS Non-Exam Schools	710	7.0%	834	21.3%	1020	16.3%
Boston Charters	347	20.7%	206	38.3%	204	27.9%

Many charter schools are mission driven to send students to college and provide sophisticated counseling and other structures to facilitate college application and enrollment processes. One Boston charter school's mission statement reads, quite simply, "our mission is to prepare every student for college." The same school, like many of its counterparts, lists a number of college readiness and support programs, employs a "director of college programming," and proudly notes that "100 percent of our graduating seniors have been accepted to colleges."[21]

But helping students get into college and equipping them to stay there are not the same thing. At first blush, even Boston's highly successful charter schools are virtually indistinguishable from their district school counterparts when it comes to college persistence rates.[22] A 2016 study found that of Boston's district, charter, and parochial high school graduates who went on to college, only about half had earned a degree within six years. These data included Boston's prestigious exam schools.[23] When the city's exam schools aren't included in the data set, more charter school students graduate from college within six years. While these data mainly suggest room for improvement for all schools, they also hint that some of the investment that Boston's charter schools make in college preparation pays off for charter students.

And there is other evidence that suggests Boston's charters have an edge when it comes to post-secondary success. One RCT study found that attendance at one of Boston's charter high schools increases the likelihood that graduates will attend a four-year rather than a two-year college. This could mean these charters are setting a higher bar for students. It could also mean they are helping students access scholarships and other resources that make four-year colleges feasible.

College persistence is one of the most important metrics for understanding the extent to which schools — all schools — are preparing students for success. Students leave college for many reasons, but a lack of preparedness and affordability top the list.[24] Within and beyond Massachusetts, there is evidence that top-performing charter networks are at the fore of tracking — often of their own volition and with their own resources — where alumni go after graduation and whether they graduate from college.[25] Emerging data suggest that top-performing networks like KIPP and Uncommon Schools are seeing alumni graduate from college at three to five times the national average.[26]

> Academy of the Pacific Rim in Boston graduated its first class in 2003. Since that time, 70 percent of its graduates have earned four-year degrees. This is far above the 2015 national average of 33.4 percent.

In the coming years, as these networks mature, they will have more robust and reliable data sets to share with one another and with public schools across the country. More importantly, these networks should also be able to provide insight into the practices they put in place and changes they made to see college going and persistence rates rise.

Beyond the Comparisons: Why Massachusetts Charters Achieve

Despite the various documented successes of charter schools in Massachusetts, they still exist in an environment that can at best be termed politically unfriendly. The expansion of charter schools has been slow and circumscribed by regulation. In 2016, the Commonwealth's voters decided overwhelmingly against lifting the charter school cap in underperforming districts.

For charter school consumers and advocates, opposition to the movement is difficult to understand. Charters serve students who haven't traditionally had access to great public schools, and data show they serve them well. What's not to like?

There are probably as many answers to that question as there are charter school detractors, but one fairly simple explanation may be that, from the beginning, charter schools have been framed in opposition to one of the most cherished institutions in the Commonwealth: public schools.

Of course, charters are public schools. They just aren't "public" as most people understand it. Students and families choose charters, they aren't always "neighborhood" schools, and charter schools generally don't unionize.

Those opposed to charters, most noticeably the state's teachers' unions, have gone to great lengths to characterize them as quasi-private schools, even "for profit."[27] So even when the data on charter public schools are clear — they perform well, they are egalitarian, they close achievement gaps for poor and minority students — those data are often overlooked or clouded by false information and half truths about charters, which are public institutions that may contract with but cannot be established by for-profit education providers or parochial schools.[28]

If charters are to serve one of their original purposes — spurring innovation, competition, and high achievement among different types of schools — then it is time to get beyond comparisons, which have been detrimental to both district and charter schools. Instead, we should look at the data and ask tough questions: Why do some charters perform so well? What can other types of schools learn from them? What do charters have to learn from other sectors?

Researchers point to a number of factors that foster success in the charter school sector. Most national charter school organizations agree that strict accountability for outcomes is essential for charter school success. Most also agree that charter schools require real autonomy if they are going to do anything other than replicate the status quo found in districts, though the autonomies that matter most are up for debate.

In Massachusetts, accountability for outcomes — as measured by the indicators discussed previously, such as test scores and graduation rates — has always mattered. Both DESE and BESE take charter school outcomes very seriously. They have rarely hesitated to close charters when they don't perform, and this has been a boon to the Massachusetts charter school sector.

Massachusetts charters also enjoy basic but meaningful autonomies, and the state has, for the most part, preserved those autonomies, even as it has increased the regulatory burden charter schools face. The most important autonomy might be the freedom that each Commonwealth charter school has to operate as an independent entity, free from the influence of any other district and its bureaucracy.[29]

Other autonomies charter schools enjoy are more important at the school level. These include freedom to control school budgets, assemble a staff, and extend the school day and year. In large part, the success of individual charter schools depends on how each uses these autonomies to meet student needs. The activities in which students engage in an extended school day might look very different from one building to another.

And there are two other important aspects of charter schooling in Massachusetts that make the Commonwealth an interesting case study for other states: Both the stringent charter school cap and the single authorizer model have simultaneously contributed to the excellence and the slow demise of the sector.

On one hand, the charter school cap has forced a very conservative approach to authorizing that has arguably enabled the proliferation of schools that produce strong academic outcomes. On the other, the cap has resulted in legislation that limits innovation and pushes talented individuals to places where there are better opportunities to open and experiment with different school models.

The single authorizer model has likewise limited innovation: As the state's main school oversight bureaucracy, DESE contributes comparatively limited resources to charter oversight and advocacy. Unlike a board responsible only for charter schools and the health of a charter sector, or even a university willing to develop and test new school models, DESE and BESE prefer a risk-averse approach to authorizing. This model has led to the establishment of a lot of highly successful charter schools, but we may never know what kinds of charter schools it has prevented.

The charter school policy environment in Massachusetts is critical to understanding the charter school landscape, and it will be discussed in greater detail in subsequent chapters. Once the nature of the environment in which charter schools operate is clear, it becomes easier to pull back the curtain and understand what the most successful charter schools in the country do to earn that label.

CHAPTER 4

Leveraging Autonomy:

How High-Performing Charter Schools Get Results

A CCOUNTABILITY FOR OUTCOMES AND A conservative approach to authorizing are two factors that have led to the success of Massachusetts's charter schools. But accountability is only one part of the charter school bargain. The Commonwealth also guarantees charter schools a great deal of autonomy — especially in comparison to other states.

The autonomies that Commonwealth charter schools have are basic but important. Charters have the ability to organize around a core mission, curricular theme, or pedagogical approach. They also control their own budgets. Perhaps most importantly, Commonwealth charter schools operate as their own school districts. This means that, unless their teachers choose to unionize, charters are not subject to the constraints of teacher collective bargaining agreements that often hamstring district schools.

Commonwealth charter schools have the autonomy to:

(1) Organize around a core mission, theme, or teaching method

(2) Control school budgets

(3) Hire (and fire) staff

The state's approach to authorizing protects these autonomies. If, for example, the Legislature had allowed school districts to authorize schools, districts could pressure charters to unionize. Unionization can adversely impact, among other things, a school leader's ability to assemble the staff of his or her choice. Collective bargaining agreements place many constraints on hiring processes, entitling more senior teachers to plum teaching positions. They can also make it difficult to extend school days and years. Nationally, school districts have reputations as poor authorizers. Most strip charter schools of autonomy, even autonomies that charters may be entitled to under law.[1]

Of course, charter school teachers don't give up their right to unionize just by agreeing to work in a charter school. Since the MERA was enacted, teachers at six Commonwealth charter schools have chosen to unionize. One of those unions disbanded as some teachers left the school and others expressed unhappiness with what they were getting from the union in exchange for dues.

In the charter school concept, the whole point of additional autonomy is that schools use it to subvert the status quo. That is exactly what the most successful charter schools do. The ways in which charter schools have taken advantage of their autonomies are too numerous to count, but they tend to fall into a few categories. Massachusetts charters:

- Create purposeful communities organized around distinct approaches to school;
- Employ time, budgets, and other resources in ways that advantage students;
- Develop targeted approaches to recruiting and developing talent;
- Challenge traditional school structures, emphasizing small schools that serve broad grade-spans

Distinctive Approaches to School

While it is true that Boston, in particular, has been home to many charter schools that take a no-excuses approach to education, the MERA gave rise to a wide variety of charters, especially in the beginning. Some of the earliest charter schools could hardly be described as no excuses. Others took a no excuses pedagogical approach but distinguished themselves by organizing around a core theme to attract students or serve a particular community.

One early example of a distinctive approach to schooling is the Francis W. Parker Charter Essential School. A member of the Coalition of Essential Schools, Parker was one of the first charter schools established in the Commonwealth. Students at Parker are not categorized by grade but by divisions. They master "conventional subject areas" (and MCAS), but they go through the curriculum in a manner different from most American schoolchildren: in multi-aged classrooms. In upper high school (11th and 12th grades) students take yearlong courses — in-depth studies of the humanities, history, and mathematics, with a faculty member as a guide.[2]

Parker uses a distinctive approach to assessment, which is one of the main things that the authors of the MERA hoped charters would do. Parker faculty do not give students traditional letter grades. Instead, working with students, they compile portfolios of student work to better assess growth over time. Portfolios allow teachers across subject areas to understand the depth and breadth of each student's work. They are very different from the "slice of time" assessments reflected by multiple choice tests, which are tools better suited for measuring the progress of large groups of students, across a sizable district, city, or state.[3]

As a part of the Coalition of Essential Learning, Parker also emphasizes specific "habits of learning." These habits are markedly different from many of those that no-excuses schools, which were established around the same time, choose to focus on. Where no-excuses schools became famous for prescribing certain behaviors ("sit up straight," "track the speaker with your eyes"), Parker faculty talk about cultivating inquiry, expression, and attentiveness in school and life. Just like a no-excuses school, Parker isn't a fit for every student. And that's the point of charter schools.

In the 1990s and into the turn of the century, the Commonwealth approved many charters that offer distinctive pedagogical approaches. Sturgis Charter School and Mystic Valley Regional Charter Academy were among the first and remain some of the few schools that offer International Baccalaureate programming for students. The Academy of the Pacific Rim in the Hyde Park neighborhood of Boston has received national recognition for its academic and character education programs, where the "individualism of the west" combines with "best practices for academic and personal development" from Pacific Rim countries.[4] These schools and others belong to a crop of charters that used their autonomy to offer innovative pedagogies.

But distinctiveness doesn't stem from pedagogical approach alone. Some charters have challenged conceptions of school structure. Codman Academy in Dorchester is an example of how schools can serve communities differently when they have the freedom to try new things.

Codman opened in 2001 adjacent to the Codman Square Health Center. The school, which has grown to serve students in grades K–12, provides a holistic program that emphasizes academics alongside the socio-emotional and physical health of students, families, and the surrounding community.[5]

Co-location with the health center allows Codman Academy to meet the needs of a diverse set of families. By leveraging health professionals and their facilities, the school pairs students and their parents/caregivers with intake counselors equipped to address non-academic issues that can affect academic performance. These include the mental and physical health of students and family members, access to healthful food, and even physical safety.[6]

This model is often referred to as "wrap-around," and it has made Codman Academy a very important part of Dorchester's Codman Square community. It has also helped Codman's students thrive academically. In 2015, *US News & World Report* awarded Codman a bronze medal on its list of "Best High Schools" in the U.S.[7]

If Parker and Codman are examples of how charters have innovated in terms of pedagogy and school structure, other Commonwealth charters have been innovative in their intentional attempts to serve underserved populations of students. Organizations such as Phoenix Charter Academies (profiled in the previous chapter) and Bridge Boston have crafted missions that help them to recruit vulnerable students: those who are homeless, who are without family members to raise them, and those who have struggled to stay in traditional schools. Other examples include Excel Academies, which in 2003 sought to fill the gap in high-quality educational opportunities for English language learners. Today, Excel Academies are seen as a model for serving families and students for whom English is a second language.[8]

Bridge Boston

Bridge Boston received its charter in 2011 to serve students in grades K–8. Bridge aims to attract the most vulnerable students in the city in Boston and provide them with supports and services that will allow them to excel academically. The school does this, in part, by trying to remove "the health and social obstacles that hinder student learning."

Each child at Bridge Boston receives regular health and dental screenings, and clinical counseling and other services are available. The school also provides a range of services for families, including parenting workshops and services that connect families to housing and employment opportunities. In addition to emphasizing a rigorous academic curriculum, Bridge Boston helps children to become and remain physically active. Instead of replacing recess with academics, Bridge ensures that students have two recess periods a day in addition to regular physical education classes.*

---

* http://bridgebostoncs.org/mission-history/

Would these schools exist if they didn't have the freedom to organize around a distinct mission or to hire the right people to fulfill that mission? Perhaps. But the path to success might have been more difficult. The Commonwealth's charter law and approach to authorizing, especially in the immediate post-education reform era, encouraged schools to experiment and differentiate themselves in ways that district bureaucracies sometimes find challenging. This is not because districts are incapable of innovation. Rather, it is because the circumstances under which districts operate make innovation more difficult.

Districts draw students based on ZIP Codes. Charters can draw students because of their attractive offerings. Leaders in district schools have to overcome considerable collective bargaining hurdles to assemble the staffs that they want. Charter schools can intentionally hire people who buy into their mission and are excited by it. These are just some of the ways that autonomy has helped Commonwealth charters provide alternatives for students who want them. And there are others.

Deploying Time, Budgets, and Other Resources Differently

Nationally, charter schools are known for extending school days and years. Massachusetts charters are no exception. The best charters deploy extra time in ways that enhance student learning and engagement. They also use budgetary autonomy to provide resources that support student and teacher time on learning.

One Massachusetts charter has been at the national forefront of rethinking how students spend their time in schools. This organization prioritizes a highly personalized approach to learning for students. It also prioritizes sharing what it has learned with schools across the Commonwealth and the nation.

Match Charter Public High School first experimented with "high-dosage tutoring" in 2002.[9] Eager to help students master and then go beyond MCAS, the school started by providing a

Academy of the Pacific Rim

Academy of the Pacific Rim (APR), located in the Hyde Park neighborhood of Boston, was one of the first Boston charter schools to receive national recognition for its innovative approach to school. In 2014, *US News and World Report* called it one of the best high schools in the United States. Pacific Rim earned this recognition because of its rigorous academic program and its approach to character education, which academics and reporters from around the country have profiled.

Pacific Rim's character education and academic curriculum borrows from several different east Asian cultures. Students learn Mandarin in high school and many participate in one of two exchange programs in China. Every year 15–20 APR students travel with school chaperones to a sister school in Beijing, China for two weeks. A smaller subset of students participates in a 12-week study abroad experience. APR also hosts students and teachers from Beijing. To travel to China, students must display a "consistent work ethic and strength of character" in school. The study abroad experience is such an important part of Pacific Rim's culture that the school builds much of the expense into its budget. Families that can pay 45 percent of total trip expenses. Financial aid is available for those who cannot afford the expense.[*]

group of sophomores with math tutors. But the model wasn't tutoring as usual: Instead of well-intentioned volunteers from all walks of life, Match sought college graduates who were top of their class. Match paid the tutors a stipend (supplemented in part by a federal grant), and carefully designed a tutor training program, in collaboration with teachers, to ensure that all the adults working with students were aligned in their approach.

That first year, each tutor had one to three students in his or her charge. Sophomore math scores grew so much during the pilot tutoring program that Match leadership became convinced tutoring was a powerful whole-school intervention. They began

[*] http://www.pacrim.org/apps/pages/index.jsp?uREC_ID=88709&type=d

to explore how to integrate tutoring into the school day and into the overall pedagogical approach at Match.

The challenge, as Match founder Michael Goldstein describes it, was how to pay for a high-quality tutor for every student in every subject. He envisioned something similar to AmeriCorps, with full-time volunteers who committed to one year with Match and worked for a small stipend. Goldstein's vision came to fruition as the Match Corps. By raising philanthropic funding at the outset, Match was able to build an entire tutoring program and integrate tutoring into every student's school day.

To keep costs down over time, the school built a dormitory where tutors lived. In that first year of Match Corps, tutors earned a $13,000 to $15,000 stipend — an amount that made living in the city of Boston or anywhere nearby impossible. Having tutors on site solved the housing issue. It also had other benefits. Because they lived on site, tutors were available throughout the school day. They were also integrated members of the school's culture, known to students, teachers, and administrators alike.

The tutor corps model that Match initiated in 2002 has come to be the backbone of Match's approach to school.[10] Today, Match Corps operates on four important pillars: 1) Hire bright young people to commit to tutoring for a year; 2) Fully integrate tutoring into the life of the school; 3) Provide a strong accountability system to ensure tutor effectiveness; and 4) Establish strong relationships among teachers, tutors, parents, and students.

When Match says, "hire bright young people," they mean it. Tutoring at Match is a competitive gig, somewhat akin to being accepted to Teach for America. The program draws graduates from the nation's top universities. Once admitted to the Corps, tutors undergo intense training. They also work closely with teachers to understand content and any challenges that students are facing. Teachers and school leaders constantly provide tutors feedback on their work. In the Match model, all adults in the building are accountable for student growth.

Match Corps has helped Match's schools produce astounding results. It can be difficult to disentangle the effects of tutoring

The Four Pillars of Match Corps

(1) Hire bright young people

(2) Fully integrate tutoring into the life of the school

(3) Provide a strong accountability system to ensure tutor effectiveness

(4) Establish strong relationships among teachers, tutors, parents, and students

from the effects of other school practices, but Match realized a substantial increase in student achievement pre- and post-Match Corps. A quasi-experimental analysis performed in 2013 found that "on average extended learning time (ELT) tutorials at Match Charter Public High School raised student achievement on the 10th grade English language arts examination between .15 and .25 standard deviations per year. That is equivalent to approximately an additional year's worth of instruction."[11]

Match's success with high-dosage tutoring is in large part due to the budgetary and other freedoms it has as a charter school. Match Corps is now an integrated part of each Match school's budget. Prioritizing tutoring is something the organization can do because it has complete control of the public dollars it receives and the philanthropic money it raises. And Match's ability to extend the school day and year allows it to leverage time to its advantage. Tutors can work with students before, during, and after school. They can train on Match's (shorter) summer breaks and support students during the extended school year.

This is not to suggest that districts can't benefit from and implement the Match approach. Innovations born of charter autonomy should be and, in the case of Match, are relevant in other contexts.

With Match's support, several Boston charter schools have

adapted the Match tutoring approach, and the Lawrence Public Schools have deployed Match-style tutoring as part of an overall approach to district turnaround. Schools and districts in other states, such as Texas and Illinois, have done the same.[12]

Match is not the only Massachusetts charter organization that has leveraged time and budgetary autonomy to the advantage of students. A great number of charter schools start the school year early (up to one month earlier than districts) and end it late. At Mystic Valley Regional Charter School in Malden, an extended day and school year allow students more time on task to access a curriculum that starts with a Core Knowledge approach and culminates with an International Baccalaureate degree. Providing students with more time to learn, when that time is focused and other resources are properly deployed to support it, provides greater access and equity for students.[13]

Recruiting and Cultivating Teacher Talent

Most charter school leaders will say that the autonomy they can't do without is the ability to assemble their own staffs. The most successful schools prioritize excellent teaching.

Research on teacher impacts consistently finds that good teachers make all the difference in student outcomes, even when other resources are lacking or unavailable. When "effective teaching" is defined as the extent to which a teacher helps students grow on standardized assessments, students assigned to effective teachers are "more likely to go on to college, earn higher incomes, and less likely to be teenage mothers."[14] According to one study, having an effective teacher, no matter a student's social background, "raises his or her cumulative life income by $80,000."[15]

Highly effective, experienced teachers sometimes present themselves at the schoolhouse door. They might transfer from another school or district for personal or professional reasons. Research shows that wealthy suburban districts attract the most effective teachers because they can pay them more.

Charter schools in urban centers can rarely compete with the pay that large districts — suburban or urban — offer. This is one reason why many charters have developed programs and processes for cultivating effective teachers. Investing in less experienced teachers who are reflective and willing to learn also allows charters more freedom to prioritize hiring people who buy into their distinct school missions.

Because the vast majority of charter schools are not unionized, school leaders can select from a wider range of candidates than their peers in district settings who are beholden to collective bargaining agreements. And charter leaders often widen the teacher candidate net in another way: They look beyond traditional teacher preparation programs in search of candidates. Many prefer to hire young people from strong universities with Bachelor's degrees in relevant content areas. The Commonwealth's several routes to teacher licensure make this possible; applicants with a Bachelor's degree who have passed the Massachusetts Test for Educator Licensure (MTEL) can receive a preliminary license to teach in public schools.[16]

But charters don't simply hire bright young people and put them in front of children. The best schools craft sophisticated approaches to teacher induction and development specific to their missions, pedagogical philosophies, and student needs. When teacher training programs work well, school leaders solve for two needs at once: They acculturate new teachers to the work and life of the school and impart effective teaching practices specific to the individual school context.

The robust on-the-job training programs that many charter organizations offer are attractive to young people because they open up a career path that some might not have considered in college. Match, for example, offers a teacher corps that is a logical extension of its tutor corps. Some tutors discover that they enjoy and are good at teaching and go on to apply to Match's teacher induction program. Tutors selected for the teacher corps go through a year of rigorous training (while they tutor!) that includes long classes on weekends and a teacher apprentice-ship model. Prospective teachers advance from simulated class-room experiences to the real thing, all while receiving targeted, in-the-moment coaching and feedback from experienced Match faculty.

Other charters also take an apprenticeship approach. Edward Brooke, recognized by the Education Trust as one of the best schools — charter, public, or private — in the nation, recruits teacher apprentices into a very competitive "associate teacher program." Associate teachers "participate in targeted profes-sional development and co-planning sessions with experienced teachers," as they slowly take on more and more responsibility. For Brooke, "growing its own" is a priority. The organization focuses on cultivating all teachers, whether novice or experi-enced, "every day."[17]

Whether they grow their own or partner with outside organizations — even universities — high-performing charters, like Brooke, all view teacher development as a long-term invest-ment. Ongoing, high-quality professional development is a way to ensure results for students and to retain the talent that will ultimately train the next crop of new teachers. Much like the data-driven approach to assessment that many adopted early on, the highest performing charters are also known for feedback and growth-oriented teacher evaluation systems. David Osborne of the Progressive Policy Institute has noted that one reason for the strong results charters achieve is that "principals, deans, and teacher leaders spend a great deal of time observing teachers and giving them feedback, often more than once a week."[18]

This culture of teacher training and development is a main reason why charters can have less experienced staff and still realize excellent results. Data show that more than 50 percent of teachers in Boston-area charters are 32 years old or younger and a large percentage of those teachers are younger than 26. In Boston Public Schools, the majority of teachers are older than 32.

Young charter school teachers are also highly educated. A 2015 random sample of the teaching staff at Boston Collegiate Charter School showed 86 percent of teachers included had degrees from "selective" or "highly selective" universities, according to *US News & World Report*. This number is high in comparison to Boston Public Schools, where a 2010 study found that only two-thirds of teachers held degrees from such institutions.

The educational background of charter school teachers may be one reason why so many of them, though young, quickly become highly effective. Considering that charter school salaries are not very competitive in Massachusetts, it is even more impressive that charter schools achieve such outsized results for students.

Charters pay their teachers (on average) considerably less than district public schools. In 2016–2017, the average teacher salary in the Boston Public Schools, a large unionized district with a lengthy collective bargaining agreement, was $90,000. A *Boston Globe* payroll review found that the same year, teachers in Boston's charter schools made an average of $55,000.

This disparity arises in part because charter school teachers are, on average, younger and less experienced than their BPS peers. But charter school teachers report that some of the other benefits of working in their schools — such as mission-driven cultures and ongoing investments in professional growth — are great incentives to work in the charter sector.[19]

Finding talent that is willing to trade salary for other benefits isn't easy and, over time, it can be difficult to convince charter school teachers to stay. In large East Coast urban centers it can be difficult to support a family on the average charter school pay. This is one reason why charters have slightly higher teacher turnover than surrounding districts.[20]

Often unable to pay teachers more because of constrained budgets (see chapter 5), charter schools choose to invest heavily in the hiring and teacher induction processes that will help teachers to become effective quickly. Understanding whether a candidate is a solid investment isn't always easy. It takes time to discover whether an individual is a fit for the culture of an organization, and in many charter schools the culture is one of long hours and very hard work. Charter school leaders describe their hiring processes as very intentional. Many view hiring as a way to understand the "extent to which a candidate's educational ideals and vision align with the institution's ideals and vision."[21]

Of course, in some cases, "fit" doesn't trump pay, especially when candidates have a rare skill set. In these circumstances, charter schools also have some leverage, because they have budgetary autonomy. Given their missions or student populations, some schools place a premium on teachers with certain expertise, such as advanced math, science, or even special education qualifications. Charters have the autonomy to pay such candidates more, and they can make salary decisions with considerably less difficulty than their district counterparts.

Autonomies like these allow charters to be nimble and responsive to programmatic needs in ways that they might not otherwise be. When used well, they foster success.

Rethinking School Structures

Some successful charter schools, like Codman Academy, have built school structures around specific missions. But the success of Massachusetts charters has elicited a broader conversation about traditional school structures.

Grown from the ground up, with space and budgets constrained by a lack of facilities funding, the vast majority of charters in the country and the Commonwealth are comparatively small schools. The largest charter organizations enroll between 1,500 and 2,000 students, usually across 12 grades, and sometimes on multiple campuses. Most charter schools in the Commonwealth have maximum enrollment capacity between 500 and 1,000 students across grades 6–12. Many charters can accommodate even fewer students.[22]

The small size of charters provides several benefits. Students express feeling "known" to everyone. With fewer teachers to train and leaner administrative teams, the adults in each building are also known to one another.[23] This is not to suggest that small size makes everything better. Charters have difficulty creating economies of scale when offering programs. They may be less likely to have robust extracurricular offerings, such as competitive sports. But when it comes to school culture and academics, small schools tend to be tight-knit communities where instruction is more easily personalized.

Research supports the relationship between small schools and effectiveness. Small schools 1) raise student achievement, 2) increase attendance, 3) increase teacher satisfaction, and 4) lead to improved school climate. This can be especially true for socioeconomically disadvantaged students.[24] The popularity of small schools in districts, especially large urban districts, has increased over time as small charter schools have proven effective. Boston Public Schools have split some larger schools into several schools within one building. Communities like Chelsea have done the same.

Whether intentionally or fortuitously, charter schools have also shone a light on the effectiveness of keeping cohorts of students together, often under the same roof, for long periods of time. In the more than 20 years of the charter school movement in Massachusetts, charters have grown vertically, rather than horizontally. Organizations that were once high school only have established middle schools. Organizations that were middle school only have established elementary schools. Organizations that began as elementary schools have also "grown up," establishing their own high schools.

Sometimes these schools keep students in close proximity to one another, but in many cases they establish multiple campuses. By adding grade levels as opposed to replicating schools that serve the same grades, these charters are meeting perceived community needs.

Charter leaders, especially leaders of charter middle and high schools, note that when students come to them they require extra time and attention to catch up to grade level — families seek charters when they aren't satisfied with the public system. Several studies support the idea that charter schools in Boston and many other urban centers are expert in catching students up. CREDO at Stanford University finds that urban Massachusetts charters, on average, add roughly 40 days of additional learning per year in math and 28 additional days of learning per year in reading."[25]

By expanding to lower grades, charters are attempting to prevent students from falling behind in the first place. "If we can serve them early," they assume, students will have more opportunity for exposure to higher-level learning. By establishing high schools, they are giving students that have grown with them for years the opportunity to flourish in a rigorous academic setting.

Creating new schools and grade levels is no easy feat. When Edward Brooke opened its first high school in the 2016–17 school year, it did so after serious consideration and with eyes wide open. Administrators and teachers thought deeply about how they would have to adapt their very structured programming for high school students who need to learn to operate in the world more autonomously. They considered with great intentionality the difference between sending someone to eighth grade and sending someone to college.[26]

Serving students from "cradle to college" is an approach more often found in the private school than public school sector, but charter schools are once again highlighting its value. If students, families, and faculty feel "known" in small schools, they feel part of a deeply rooted school community when they are in those schools for 12 to 13 years.

Sticking with students for so long has risks, of course: Would a student have flourished differently elsewhere? Does a small school provide students with enough exposure to the diverse adult world they will navigate after graduation?

But the benefits of small, deep, learning communities seem to outweigh the risks. This is made evident by the great academic and other successes many charters have realized after expanding their offerings.

The tendency for charter schools to be small communities that grow vertically as opposed to horizontally is less a phenomenon born of the autonomy they have under law and more a consequence of the Massachusetts policy environment, which allows for limited charter school seats and therefore limited replication of programming. But charter schools that have expanded have remained very effective, and this effectiveness is in large part due to the autonomies that charters leverage well.

Many charter schools explicitly share best practices (see the example of Match outlined previously). But even when they don't, charters strongly influence the other public schools around them. Policymakers in Massachusetts have looked to successful charters to see what they do differently. They have also attempted to foster charter school practices in districts.

Implementing common charter school practices in district schools is possible. The Lawrence Public Schools have realized notable academic gains for students by implementing initiatives born in the charter sector (like high-dosage tutoring) without giving up teacher collective bargaining rights and other things that districts value.[27] But some charter practices, like the autonomy to hire without constraint and to have full control of school budgets, are exceedingly difficult to implement in district settings, which means districts have to adapt, rather than adopt some charter initiatives.

Charter school founders and leaders, if they are wise, will continue not only to share what they know but to look to their district peers to learn what they do well and what charters can do better. In Massachusetts, some charter schools are rethinking discipline policies by taking cues from their district peers. When these exchanges happen, both charters and district schools are at their best, fulfilling the good intent of the MERA, rather than subverting it.

CHAPTER 5

Follow the Money:

Charter School Funding and Its Impacts

A S IN MOST STATES, LOCAL AND REGIONAL school districts in Massachusetts receive about 90 percent of their funding from local property taxes and state contributions. Roughly 10 percent of funding for most schools comes in the form of grants provided by the federal government. The MERA fundamentally shifted the state's contribution to the Commonwealth's poorest school districts, establishing a "foundation budget" designed to ensure that cities and towns lacking the capacity to raise enough money to provide an "adequate" education for each student via the property tax would receive additional assistance.

> In *McDuffy v. Secretary of the Executive Office of Education*, the Massachusetts Supreme Judicial Court found that the Commonwealth has an "enforceable duty to provide an education for all its children, rich and poor, in every city and town through the public schools." The Court also found that "[w]hile it is clearly within the power of the Commonwealth to delegate some of the implementation of the duty to local governments, such power does not include a right to abdicate the obligation imposed on magistrates [the executive branch] and Legislatures placed on them by the Constitution."[*]

---

[*] *McDuffy v. Secretary of the Executive Office of Education*, 415 Mass. 545, 615 N.E.2d 516 (1993), summarized at http://www.doe.mass.edu/lawsregs/litigation/mcduffy_hancock.html.

The mechanism the MERA uses to assist localities with education funding is Chapter 70, which provides direct operating aid to school districts. Under Chapter 70, the state annually determines a "foundation budget," which is the minimum per-pupil allocation necessary to provide students with an adequate education. The foundation budget is higher for English language learners and students with special educational needs.

Once the foundation budget is set, the state calculates the minimum amount municipalities must spend (the "required local contribution"), the level of aid that will come from the state, and a minimum level of total spending that in some cases is above the foundation (required "net school spending"). Chapter 70 was progressive when it was conceived and it continues to be progressive; it requires wealthier cities and towns to contribute more to schools from their municipal budgets, and provides additional state aid to poorer areas.[1]

Foundation Budget

The foundation budget is an amount, determined by the state, that each district needs to provide an adequate education to each student. Once it establishes a foundation budget, the state determines each district's capacity to meet that budget using local revenue. The extent to which different cities and towns can meet the foundation budget varies widely, according to property tax bases. When a locality cannot reasonably raise enough revenue to operate its schools adequately, the Commonwealth provides Chapter 70 aid. The amount that the Commonwealth provides is the difference between what each locality can raise in local revenue and its pre determined foundation budget.

Although the MERA was groundbreaking in its attempt to ensure equitable funding for all students, it would prove more difficult to equitably fund students choosing to attend charter schools. When the MERA was being written, designing the charter school funding formula posed several challenges:

- Charters would be considered their own school districts for some purposes, but not for the purpose of school funding. Unable to draw from a local property tax base, charters would need another mechanism to provide per-pupil tuition;
- Charters would need facilities, but without a tax base, they would be unable to use local funds;
- Commonwealth charters were intended to provide healthy competition for districts, but legislators felt strongly that they shouldn't divert needed resources away from district schools.

In the few other states with charter laws in the 1990s, legislators addressed these issues in various ways. Some allowed districts to run charters, resulting in the sharing of facilities and resources but also limiting charter autonomy. Others allocated state funds for charter schools but funded charters at much lower rates than their district counterparts.[2]

Proponents of the Massachusetts legislation saw charters as increasing school choice for families and providing an opportunity to develop new practices that could be shared with districts. For these reasons, neither district-run charter schools nor underfunded charter schools was an option. They set out to design a charter school finance system that was comparatively equitable.

Legislators knew that charter school students would otherwise be assigned to a local school district. Under the MERA, state aid and local funds flow first through the district. The money charters receive, referred to as tuition, is meant to provide charter students with the same allocation that they would receive from the district. The law states that the tuition provided to charters by each sending district should be calculated to reflect "the actual per-pupil spending amount that would be expended in the district if the students attended the district schools." The rationale behind the law is that money be allocated for students, not schools.[3]

This does not mean that the tuition payments charters receive for each student are equal. Per-pupil allocations vary based on a student's grade level and family background — economically disadvantaged students and English language learners receive a larger per-pupil allocation in the district setting and this is reflected in charter school tuition payments. Students with other special educational needs, those who have Individualized Education Plans (IEPs), do not receive additional ("weighted") money. Instead, the funding formula assumes that charter schools educate the same proportion of these students as the sending district. This has two implications for the charter/district school relationship: 1) Charters have no financial incentive to enroll students with IEPs (as they might with other groups) and 2) when they do not enroll high numbers of these students, they are effectively receiving money to cover the costs associated with serving students with IEPs — costs that they may not face.

At first blush, the tuition formula seems not only fair but also quite generous to charter schools. However, charters face a financial burden that isn't covered by tuition: establishing and maintaining facilities.

School districts have always been able to draw upon property taxes to establish and maintain school buildings. Since 2004, they have also had an additional pool of money to access. Municipalities can access funding from the Massachusetts School Building Authority (MSBA) to build new buildings and maintain existing ones. Charters do not have access to these funds.

Charters do receive a small facilities stipend from the state; it is folded into the tuition payment districts make to charters. There are two noteworthy things about the facilities payment. First, districts are supposed to be reimbursed for this spending through the charter school reimbursement formula (discussed below). Second, the facilities payment is not enough to establish and maintain charter schools, so charters must raise large sums of money — mainly from philanthropists — just to survive.[4]

In recent years, the facilities payment has been about $893 per pupil. This sounds like a lot, until we consider what the average charter school looks like. If a charter school serves 210 students, 30 students in each grade, 6 through 12, it would receive about

$187,000 for facilities. The cost of real estate in Massachusetts is very high, and even higher in the urban communities where charter school demand is highest. In most cases, $187,000 annually covers only a very small portion of facilities costs. Charters must include facilities costs in their overall budget, and most spend an additional $500 per pupil beyond their facilities allocation just to keep the lights on.[5] Unless this funding comes from outside sources, it can cut into money that might otherwise go to staff, students, and/or instructional time.

Historically, charters have risen to the challenge of operating with little capital funding. As early as 1997, the first charters were using a greater portion of their budget than districts to establish and maintain facilities, yet still flourishing academically despite having less money to spend directly on education. Given their success, demand for these new schools was outstripping supply.[6]

Due to that demand, in 1997 the Legislature raised the state cap on charter schools slightly. At the same time, it revised the funding formula to ameliorate some of the "pain" districts were experiencing as more and more students left for charters.

Under the formula, the state reimbursed districts for annual increases in charter school tuition. If a district saw more students leave for a charter school in 1998 than 1997, the state reimbursed the district for the increase in tuition. For the first year, districts were reimbursed 100 percent of the total tuition increase. In the second and third years, districts were reimbursed for 60 and 40 percent of the total increase, respectively.[7]

The new formula recognized that when school districts, which can be large bureaucracies, lose pupils, they are often unable to "right size" operations right away. Schools have to keep the lights on and determine how many teachers they will need (which depends on class sizes), among other things.

As more students began to leave districts for charters in the late 1990s, districts complained that the tuition that followed charter school students was negatively impacting their day-to-day operations. While critics charged that districts should adjust to lower enrollment — as they might when students move or go to a private school — districts and teachers' unions accused char-

Flow of Funds to Local School Districts

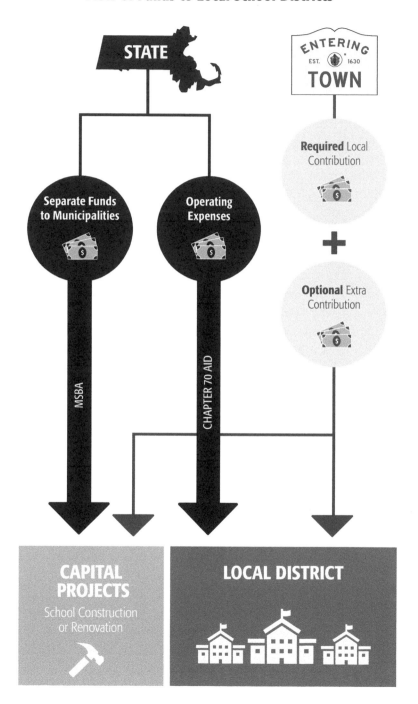

Flow of Funds to Charter Schools

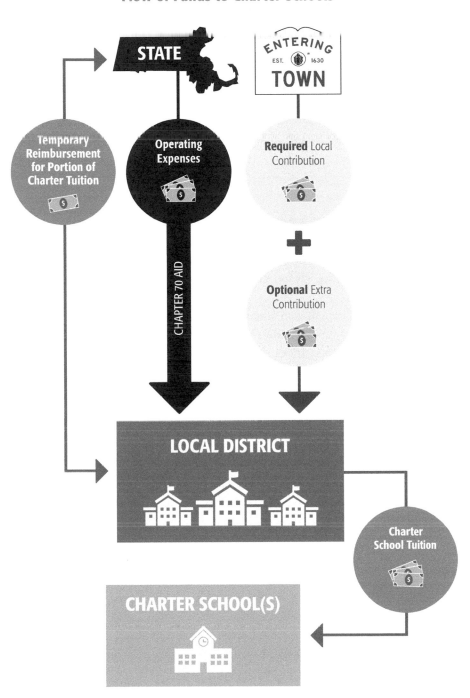

District Reimbursements for
Charter School Tuition Over Time[8]

	Prior Year Tuition	Current Year Tuition	Change in Tuition	Amount Reimbursed
Year 1	0	$100,000	$100,000	$100,000
Year 2	$100,000	0	($100,000)	$25,000
Year 3	0	0	0	$25,000
Year 4	0	0	0	$25,000
Year 5	0	0	0	$25,000
Year 6	0	0	0	$25,000

Districts receive $225,000 in exchange for a one time, $100,000 tuition payment to charters.

ters of "draining" resources from the students who didn't leave for charters.

The argument continues, even two decades later. In recent years, the state has adjusted the reimbursement formula to give districts even more time to adjust when they lose pupils to charter schools. The formula is still based on changes in charter school tuition, as opposed to specific enrollment numbers, but reimbursements are doled out over six years. As the table above shows, the first year that a district pays tuition to charter schools, it is reimbursed for 100 percent of the payment. For the five years after that reimbursement, districts receive 25 percent of the increase in tuition, which means that by the end of the sixth year, the district will have received 225 percent of the initial increase in aid."[9]

Over the past decade, the Commonwealth of Massachusetts has reimbursed districts roughly $900 million for students they are not educating. In effect, it pays per-pupil tuition for charter students twice: once to the charter school and again to the district.

Charter proponents and districts in other states view Massachusetts charter school funding as a model. Not only do charters receive more generous funding than their counterparts in other states, the reimbursement formula protects districts from suffering the consequences of precipitous enrollment drops Because of this, the Commonwealth's recent, often hostile debate over whether to raise the charter cap — Question 2 — confounded many national observers.

One of the main contentions of those opposed to raising the charter school cap was that charters drain funding from local districts. The opposition, funded almost entirely by the MTA, asked the electorate to "save our public schools," from the growth of charters and the drain on resources they represent. The electorate bought this argument and voted resoundingly against raising the cap. While funding was not the only aspect of the cap-lift debate, it played a large role. But how could the opposition convince voters that charters drain resources from public schools when this claim seems so far from the truth?[10]

The answer lies both in perceptions about charter schools and the reality of how an opaque school finance system operates in practice. Confusion stems not only from a complex law but also from the experience of some districts that lose students to charters. In brief, the charter school funding formula doesn't always work the way legislators theorized it would.

Charter School Funding — In Theory

Chapter 70 funding and where it goes can be difficult to follow. Adding charter school tuition to the equation further complicates matters. Charters do not receive state aid directly. Instead, students who attend charters are counted in the local or regional district enrollment. In most school districts, these charter school students generate additional state aid, but because Chapter 70 does not segregate that aid, it can appear as though only the locality (district), not the state, is contributing to charter school tuition. This lack of transparency in the funding formula can lead to overestimates of the net impact charter schools have on many districts. In poorer districts that receive more Chapter 70 state aid — the same districts where charter schools are concentrated — the amount of local funding diverted to charters can be greatly exaggerated.

The amount of state aid generated by one additional student under Chapter 70 depends on several factors, and it could range from a low of $25 to a high of more than $13,000. Some of the differences in aid reflect the characteristics of a specific student, such as whether she is an English language learner or from a low-income family.[11] However, the primary reason for differing aid amounts is that Chapter 70 calculates aid based on a measure of the district's need.[12]

Approximately 100 districts across Massachusetts are foundation aid districts. Schools in these localities receive the largest amount of state aid. Especially when student enrollment rises, the required local contribution and the level of state aid from the previous fiscal year may be too low to ensure that every child is adequately funded, according to the state's definition. In these cases, additional state aid ensures that the district can meet the minimum per-pupil funding level.

But a locality's inability to raise enough funds is not the only reason it might become a foundation district. In some cases, student enrollment spikes in a district in a short period of time. When this happens, the foundation budget — the money needed to serve all students — exceeds the predetermined local contribution. For these districts, one extra student will generate from $7,000 to $13,000 per year, depending on the student's characteristics (low-income students, for example, will command a higher per-pupil rate). The state effectively bears the entire incremental cost to reach the minimum spending level, and the required local contribution from the student's home city or town does not change. In these foundation aid districts, state aid covers almost the entire cost of a student's education.

And even if a district is "above foundation," or can generate enough property tax revenue to meet the required local contribution, the state, in theory, should still help it fund students. The state identifies a target amount that it will pay each district, known as "target aid." Target aid from the state can range from 17 percent of the foundation budget to over 80 percent. The state is meant to pay a higher share of the budget in low-income communities and in communities with lower property values.

Unfortunately, there is a gap between policy and practice. Target aid is typically the last type of aid the state pays. In some years the state only budgets enough to pay a portion of target aid. In other years, it pays nothing at all.

And even if districts do receive their target share of state aid, if student enrollment increases and the district is "above foundation," most districts will receive little funding for additional students. In some cases, the state will pay only $25 in "minimum aid" per student, leaving the city or town to bear virtually the entire incremental cost of educating newcomers.

Of course, what the state should pay, especially in districts that are able to meet the foundation budget with local contributions, is open to debate. Should the state's priority be to focus only on the neediest districts, or does it have an obligation to provide something for everyone? The situation in Boston, which

District Funding and Charter Tuition in Boston, FY 2016

Local District	Amount (millions)	Per Pupil
Required Local Contribution	$657	$10,240
State Aid	$212	$3,310
Minimum Spending	**$870**	**$13,550**

Charter Schools	Amount (millions)	Per Pupil
Tuition (Operating)	$136	14,740
Tuition (Capital)	$8	$890
Tuition (Total)	**$145**	**$15,630**

	Amount (millions)	Per Pupil
Reimbursement – Calculated	**$41**	**$4,410**
Reimbursement – Actual	**$25.5**	**$2,750**
Reimbursement – Shortfall	**($15)**	**($1,660)**

is a non-foundation district, sheds some light on these questions.

In 2017, the required local contribution in Boston was over $650 million, and the district received $212 million in state aid. But because Boston is "above foundation," state aid does not vary with enrollment. From one perspective, the state's contribution covers 24 percent of the overall cost of education in Boston. From another, the state's overall contribution is actually much lower, because as new students enroll and the state does not adjust its contribution, districts are forced to bear the incremental increase in cost.

When only a handful of new students enter a district, the incremental cost might be bearable. Schools, for example, don't need to hire new teachers or staff for one additional pupil. But when enrollment spikes suddenly, school and district resources are stretched thin in the absence of additional funding.

What does this have to do with charter schools? Depending on one's perspective, the practice of a predetermined per-pupil allocation following each student to a charter school may or may not be "fair" to the district. In the past decade, many of the large urban communities that are home to concentrations of charter schools have seen dramatic enrollment increases. As both enrollment and the foundation budget rise, localities cannot generate the revenue needed to support the additional students. It becomes easy to blame the financial squeeze districts feel on the charter schools to which they are required to send tuition.

Moreover, if we consider non-foundation districts, in which funding does not rise with enrollment, sending tuition to charter schools feels even more controversial. When a student who lives in Boston enrolls in one of the city's charter schools, is she a pupil who was considered in the state's "target aid" allocation, or part of an overall spike in enrollment for which the district received little to no additional funding? In other words, has the state already paid 24 percent of the cost of educating that student or has it contributed nothing? Either way, the charter that the student chooses to attend will receive the full per-pupil amount that the state determines to be adequate.

And districts also cite inequities that stem from the law governing charter school enrollment. Charter schools are not required to accept new students past a certain point in the year, which means they don't encounter unmanageable spikes in enrollment. Even if the law did require charters to accept new students throughout the year, many charters are small and operating at capacity. Remember, the cap ensures that only a given number of charter school seats can exist in each district.

In theory, the tuition reimbursement districts receive when they lose students to charters should offset the cost of the full per-pupil tuition payment that districts must make to charters. In reality, the state does not always fully fund the reimbursement, which is subject to appropriation. In FY 15 and 17, for example, reimbursements were woefully underfunded, providing ammunition for the claim that charters harm districts. Of course, the reimbursement formula is only one part of the charter school funding formula. But because reimbursements are clearly tied to the money that districts pay to charters, they are easier for the pubic to understand.

As long as charter school enrollment remains at capacity, the payments districts make to charters will continue to rise. When the state does not fully fund reimbursements, some districts — those that are "above foundation" — will experience a negative financial impact, despite being fully or partially reimbursed for students they no longer educate. This does not mean, however, that the net impact of charter schools on district finances is great. With some changes to the charter school funding formula, the Commonwealth would likely be able to fulfill its intention of funding students equitably no matter what type of school they choose to attend and ensuring that districts are generously compensated for students lost to charter schools.

The Financial Impact of Charters — In Practice

When people think about the impact of charter schools, the most common scenario they think about probably involves a student enrolled in a traditional local school who switches to a charter school. The immediate impact of students leaving districts for charters is illustrated in the previous pages.

In foundation aid districts, the state pays almost the entire cost of educating the student and state aid is roughly equal to the tuition payment. However, this does not mean the sending district is not affected — it still loses tuition payments that it would otherwise not have to make. If schools or districts face significant fixed costs, the loss of students to charter schools could negatively affect schools after the initial year of full reimbursement. Over time, however, schools should be able to adjust and right-size their operations to fit budgetary realities.

But charters aren't the only reason why students leave districts. If a student moves from one district to another, or goes to a private school instead of a charter, the district is likely to suffer more. In this scenario, the district is not reimbursed for the student who leaves and will not receive Chapter 70 aid. In a foundation aid community, a student leaving for a charter school may have less impact than a student moving out of the district or enrolling in private school (or even a student who graduates from high school). Charter critics rarely consider this scenario when making the claim that charters are a financial drain on districts; few would argue that a district should be reimbursed for a student who graduates or moves out of state!

The situation is somewhat different if the student did not attend a local school before enrolling in a charter. In this scenario, the district is required to pay tuition when the student enrolls in the charter school, but it will not receive Chapter 70 aid until that student has attended the charter for a year. The reimbursement covers the entire cost of the charter student's education during the first year, after which foundation aid covers most of the cost. The reimbursement then stops, and the local district doesn't face any lingering fixed costs. Because there is no change in the number of students in the district in this scenario, and the increase in state aid is approximately equal to the increase in tuition, the district should feel no financial impact from the "loss" of a student to a charter.

In districts that do not receive foundation aid, the results are different. In these districts, tuition does not depend on state aid, meaning that a student leaving for a charter school results in the same diversion of funds away from the local schools as in a foundation aid district. Had the student remained in the district, enrollment would not change and the district would keep the tuition payment. Paying tuition to a charter becomes a "drain" if the district faces significant fixed costs.

Unlike their foundation district peers, when a student leaves an above-foundation district for another district or a private school, the district loses enrollment but not a significant amount of state aid. On the other hand, when a student leaves the same district for a charter school, its funding is reduced by the amount of local tuition it must pay. But even in this scenario, the impact on the schools again depends on the extent to which schools or districts face fixed costs. If costs are mostly variable, they will fall when the student leaves for a charter school. If costs are fixed, the local district is squeezed by tuition payments.

These scenarios suggest that the real financial impact of charters on districts is actually quite small. But what do the data show? Actual patterns of enrollment, revenue, tuition, and spending are revealing, especially since enrollment in Massachusetts's charters has risen sharply over the past decade.

Charters tend to concentrate in urban centers, due to demand and because of the 2010 legislation, which lifted the cap in underperforming districts. As a result, growth in the sector has not been equally distributed. In recent years, roughly half the districts that saw a large increase in the number of pupils leaving for charters were classified as foundation districts. Because state aid essentially pays tuition for each pupil enrolled in these districts, including those who leave for charters, the impact on roughly half the local districts with the greatest charter school enrollment is negligible.

In the other 50 percent of districts that saw growth in the charter sector — districts that are above foundation — it is useful to compare district and charter school spending to understand whether districts are "suffering" and charters "profiting" from the state's funding formula. In 2017, the most recent year for which data are available, tuition paid to charters by districts accounted for only roughly 80 percent of overall charter school spending. The remaining 17 percent came from government grants, private donors, and other fundraising efforts.

Because the average charter school spends about $2,000 per pupil on facilities and space (more than double the $893 per-pupil facilities payment the state provided in 2017), capital expenses are a large line item for these schools. This means that charters usually spend significantly less on operating expenses than their district counterparts. In 2014, charters spent roughly $800 per pupil less than their surrounding districts on operating expenses. Charters do this, in general, by paying teachers less and contributing to teachers' health benefits and retirement at much lower rates than their district counterparts. Charters have to make such trade-offs not only because of the cost of establishing and maintaining facilities, but also because their small size means more overhead and higher per-pupil administrative costs than in districts.

Despite these disparities in charter and district spending, especially on key operating expenditures such as teacher salaries, charters produce academic outcomes that are superior to those in most sending districts. Even with comparatively generous state funding, they are proving that "less is more" when it comes to per-pupil spending and student achievement.

In districts that do not receive foundation aid, the results are different. The data suggest that the actual impact of charter schools on districts is very small, and that any negative impact tends to be concentrated on a few above-foundation localities that have experienced large influxes of students in recent years. These impacts, however, are not due to charters receiving more generous funding. Instead, they are mainly caused by small flaws in the funding formula and quirks in the charter school law that leave certain payments, such as tuition reimbursements, vulnerable to cuts, as they are considered and appropriated every year by the Legislature.

Lessons Learned about Charter School Funding

As with most aspects of charter schooling in Massachusetts, whether one views charter school funding as fair comes down to how one views charter schools and funding for schools more generally. People who value the right of families to choose the schools their children attend are inclined to see state money for education as attached to a child rather than a school. Others place more emphasis on the school district as a public good, and are hesitant to allow individual choice to impact the collective resources of community and/or the status quo in any way.

In both scenarios, however, charter schools remain public schools, open to any who wish to attend. Charters exist to serve communities, but, unlike districts, they have no direct mechanism to derive funding from the community. Because charters cannot access local property tax revenue, they must rely on funding mechanisms conceived by the state.

In the vast majority of industrialized nations, schools are integral to local communities but not supported by local property taxes. In many cases this means that the quality of schools is not necessarily dependent upon the wealth of the local community (as it is in most U.S. states). It also means that local bureaucratic entities, such as school districts, have no monopoly on public education.

One of the most interesting aspects of the U.S. charter school debate is the extent to which charter schools — public schools

Charter schools are public schools.

Do we believe that school funding should be attached to families and children who have the right to choose the public school they attend? Or, do we believe that funding belongs to schools, districts, and the adults that operate them? These questions are at the heart of most controversies surrounding charter public schools.

that act as alternatives to districts — are viewed as the enemies of school districts. There are very few instances across the country where charter schools can fairly be said to drain resources from traditional school districts. As this analysis shows, Massachusetts charters have, in reality, little to no financial impact on their district counterparts.

This acknowledged, there are some aspects of charter school funding in Massachusetts that are worthy of emulation and others that are not. There are also small changes that could be made to the charter school funding formula that should put to rest any debate over the net financial impact of charters on districts.

One proposal is to leave local school districts out of the equation entirely and have the state allocate funds directly to charter schools. This would effectively make charter schools subject to appropriations. Like the reimbursements districts are supposed to receive when they lose students to charters, this would make charter school funding particularly vulnerable to budget cuts and undermine the intent of the MERA to ensure that all public school students receive equal access to a high-quality education. This would also unfairly release localities from the responsibility to contribute to the education of all citizens in a community. When residents pay a property tax, they do so with the understanding that some of that tax will be used for their children's public school education.

A better proposal may be to make the overall system of

Lessons Learned

(1) Make Funding More Transparent

(2) Weight Funding for All Schools to
Reflect Student Need

(3) Provide Charters With
Equal Facility Funding

(4) Carefully Consider Impacts of
Reimbursement Formula

school finance more transparent. Short of doing away with a system that relies on the property tax, the Commonwealth could more clearly link school funding to enrollment. In above-foundation districts, an appropriate state allocation (rather than a minimum $25 per pupil) when enrollment rises would offset the pain of paying full charter school tuition for students who choose charters even when the district is being stretched thin by rapid increases in the student population.

Providing additional (or weighted) funds for students with special educational needs could also make the overall system more fair and give charter schools additional incentives to continue enrolling these students. When districts enroll more special education students than charters and do so without additional support from the state, they face comparatively higher costs, even when they are able to provide special education services "at scale."

These changes could make charter school funding seemingly less painful for districts. Likewise, ensuring that charter schools receive an equitable facilities allocation could make the system less painful for charter schools. Although charters tend to achieve excellent outcomes even with comparatively less money to allocate for operations, they could arguably do more for students and communities if they did not have to budget so heavily for building and maintenance costs and/or raise philanthropic funds just to house students. Capital expenses are a drag on charter school budgets, eating into the educational resources they can provide for students.

One of the main features of Massachusetts's charter school funding formula that other states should emulate is the Commonwealth's commitment to providing all students — district and charter — with the same per-pupil allocation. Although the facilities burden charters face can encroach on each school's per-pupil budget, the Commonwealth comes closer than almost any other state to providing equitable funding for charter schools.

The reimbursement districts receive when they lose students to charters could also be a feature of the formula that is worthy of emulation, if only because it ensures that districts can cover fixed costs when they lose a large number of students to charters in a short period of time.

States might want to consider, however, shortening the duration of the reimbursement, so districts have an incentive to right-size budgets and operations. They might also consider the consequences of leaving this part of the charter school funding formula to the annual discretion of lawmakers. The reimbursement formula may be the most transparent aspect of charter school funding in Massachusetts; when it is underfunded, districts lose out on the money they depend on and charters lose politically because of the appearance (though it is not reality) that they are draining districts of tuition.

CHAPTER 6

A Losing Proposition:

The Best Charter Schools in the Nation V. The Status Quo

C HARTERS HAVE ALWAYS BEEN A CONTENTIOUS topic of public debate, but it wasn't until 2016 that any issue surrounding charter schools was on the ballot. Until that time, every small raise of the charter school cap, every revision to the funding formula, and every new rule governing charter schools had been decided first by the Legislature and then, in interpretation and implementation, by the BESE and the DESE.

Charter advocates in the Commonwealth may acknowledge that the cap on charter schools has played a role in ensuring quality, but they have long been keen to lift the cap and provide more families access to excellent schools. In fact, what is often referred to as "the cap" is two different caps. While the sector has room to expand under the statewide cap of 120 charter schools, a cap on the amount of tuition that individual districts can spend on charter schools means that there aren't enough charters to meet demand in some places. In 2016, places like Boston had little room for more charters, and advocates were restless.

Between 2014 and 2016 charter advocates pushed for a cap-lift in three different areas: the legislature, the courts, and the ballot box. A legislative attempt to lift the cap in 2014 made it through the House but faced opposition in the Senate, ultimately failing to pass by a wide margin.[1] Another effort passed the Senate in early 2016 but included provisions that charter supporters believed would hamper the movement — ultimately, the charter lobby convinced the House not to take up the bill.[2]

In the midst of both legislative attempts, a group of charter advocates, including Pioneer Institute, Cheryl Brown Henderson, and the Black Alliance for Educational Options filed an Amicus brief on behalf of five Boston Public Schools students challenging the constitutionality of the cap. The case made its way to the Supreme Judicial Court (SJC) in 2018. The SJC acknowledged that the plaintiffs weren't receiving an adequate education, as defined by MCAS scores, but did not allow that lifting the cap on charter schools, which it called a "fundamentally political" remedy was the right remedy or within the Court's purview. It dismissed the case.[*]

Of the three routes available, many charter advocates have long contended that the ballot box is the least desirable route to lifting the cap. Certain organizations, such as Pioneer Institute, have contended since as early as 2010 that a ballot initiative was risky. However, in 2015 some were hopeful that great demand for charter schools would give their side leverage. The popularity of Governor Charlie Baker, a charter school advocate, was added incentive to put the issue to a vote.[3] Polls in 2015 and well into 2016 showed support for lifting the cap on charter schools (59 percent "Yes" to 20 percent "No"), even among Democrats (the largest voting group in Massachusetts but the party least likely to support charter schools nationally).[**]

With enough signatures to get the issue on the ballot, key stakeholders, such as Secretary of Education James Peyser, and representatives of the New York-based organization Families for Excellent Schools (FES) carefully crafted the language of what would come to be known as Question 2. Had it passed, Question 2 would have given the Board of Elementary and Secondary Education the ability to authorize up to 12 new charter schools or expansions of existing charter schools a year (statewide), with

[*] Interview with Ryan McManus, Hemenway & Barnes LLP, May 18, 2018.
[**] Data provided from a poll conducted by Democrats for Education Reform.

priority to applicants seeking to open a school in a district that performed in the bottom 25 percent for the two years prior to application.[4]

The writers of the ballot question were strategic with its language. They aimed to ruffle legislators (mostly suburban) who didn't want charter schools in their districts. The hope was to convince legislators to come to a reasonable compromise before the question was put to voters.[5]

But anti-charter forces (mainly the state's teachers' unions) suspected they could win the day at the ballot box and legislators never took up the issue. Charter detractors called their opponents' bluff, and they won.

As the campaign for "Yes on 2" got underway, Families for Excellent Schools took a clear and prominent role in setting strategy under the campaign moniker Great Schools Massachusetts.[6] FES had participated in campaigns in New York and elsewhere, but in Massachusetts they failed to form a coalition that might have led to success.

Even the usual players in Massachusetts's charter politics, such as the Massachusetts Charter Public School Association, played a less prominent role than Families for Excellent Schools. From the beginning, few pro-charter groups were comfortable

QUESTION 2:

This proposed law would allow the state Board of Elementary and Secondary Education to approve up to 12 new charter schools or enrollment expansions in existing charter schools each year. Approvals under this law could expand statewide charter school enrollment by up to 1 percent of the total statewide public school enrollment each year. New charters and enrollment expansions approved under this law would be exempt from existing limits on the number of charter schools, the number of students enrolled in them, and the amount of local school districts' spending allocated to them.

enough with the ballot initiative or with FES's involvement in the campaign to convey a strong and united front. This is in part because *FES made clear that "it wasn't going to be a partnership. It was going to be a takeover."*[7]

The opposition, in contrast, coalesced and organized supporters from the beginning. The state's two teachers' unions, the MTA and the AFT, have deep experience with political campaigns. The "No" side had a simple and clear message for the public and it persistently and clearly broadcasted that message in a variety of ways, leveraging very trusted messengers: public school teachers.

"Yes" and "No" on 2

The wording of Question 2 gave traction to the opposition, which used it to rile constituents.[8] Suburban voters, who might have ignored or even voted for a proposal that only affected urban centers, saw charter schools as a threat. The opposition hammered home the message that charters drain money from district schools, and they convinced voters that charters could open in their backyards (as unlikely as history proves this to be).

The opposition's message was disingenuous, at best. To explain how charters drain money from districts, the "No" side told voters that when districts lose students to charters they are unable to adjust fixed costs, and students suffer. They also reminded voters that the Legislature hasn't consistently or fully funded the reimbursement formula; a truth that nonetheless obscures how generous (and expensive) that formula is in the first place.[9]

For their part, the "Yes" side did very little to clarify the confusing way in which the state funds all schools, let alone charters. They relied instead on an argument that focused on every family's right to choose a school. Choice is something with which, according to polls, most voters agree.[10] But voters were ultimately unclear on the choice that charter schools represent for families.

> "We are thrilled that the Boston School Committee has joined over 150 other school committees across the state in standing up against this irresponsible ballot question that will strip our public schools of hundreds of millions of dollars and funnel it to privately-run charter schools with no local oversight or accountability."
>
> – Juan Cofield, Co-chair, "Save Our Public Schools" in *Boston Magazine*, October 6, 2016.

In a Commonwealth where only 4.7 percent of students are enrolled in charter public schools, few parents — especially those who are satisfied with their public school options — understand school choice as a pressing concern.[11] The "No" side was able to build upon this confusion with its campaign tagline "save our public schools." No matter how hard the "Yes" side fought to remind voters that charters are public schools, in the end, many claimed to understand a "Yes" vote as something that could endanger the majority of public schools in the name of only a few.

Although the content of the messages that each side chose to send to voters was important, the methods each side used to get its message out would prove more important. The "Yes" side, a loose alliance of charter supporters with an "outside" group at the helm, raised more than $20 million. It put that money largely into television ads at the expense of other messaging.

In contrast, the "No" campaign leveraged its "great organizing capacity and depth of scale," to broadcast its message in many different forms.[12] It organized teachers to answer questions at community gatherings and convinced more than 150 school committees to pass resolutions against Question 2.[13] On city and town street corners throughout the state, union members hoisted "No on 2" signs. They also wore buttons to work that read "Save Our Public Schools."

The "No" side used another grassroots tactic as well: It harnessed volunteers to make more than a million personal phone calls to constituents, especially older people who are likely to vote but less likely to get information from the Internet. According to one interviewee, the average length of those phone calls was 30 minutes.[14] The "No" side was excellent at campaigning and it benefited from disorganization and dissent among charter supporters.

As the campaign wore on, the prominent role that Families for Excellent Schools played exacerbated the "Yes" side's challenges. Charter detractors successfully framed FES as an interloper in Massachusetts's politics, and this became a running narrative in the media. The opposition also linked FES and prominent Question 2 donors, such as Walmart Inc. heir, Jim Walton, to Wall Street. According to one charter school parent and ardent "Yes on 2" campaigner, "we were slaughtered because they made it look like the people who funded our side were all about making money... like charter schools and bankers were coming to devour our community."[15]

Picking up the "No" campaign's cues, the media heavily focused on the "dark money" that the "Yes" side was bringing to Massachusetts. The media wasn't wrong to characterize the money in this way. FES, which brought more than $13 million to the campaign, did not disclose the sources of its money. In 2017 the organization paid a $425,000 fine after the Office of Campaign and Political Finance determined that it had violated campaign finance rules.[16] FES ultimately disbanded in 2018.[17]

FES's failure to play by the rules garnered it negative attention and obscured another issue that might have been discussed: The equally enormous amount of money teachers' unions were giving to the "No" campaign derived mainly from the agency fees unions raise from their teachers.

Less than 1 percent of the money raised by the "No" side came from sources other than state or national teachers' unions.[18] In Massachusetts, not many charter schools choose to unionize, but some have. The media rarely discussed whether teachers wanted their money to go to an anti-charter campaign.

Follow The Money

"Yes on 2"		"No on 2"	
Families for Excellent Schools	$13.6M	National Education Association	$5.4M
Other "dark money"	$1.2M	Massachusetts Teachers Association	$5.9M
Jim and Alice Walton	$1.8M	American Federation of Teachers	$1.8M
Private Donors	$2M	Other Local Unions	$222K
Mass Charter Organizations	$250K	Small Donors	$17K
Mass Businesses	$575K		
Smaller Private Donations	$159K		
TOTAL	**$19.5M**		**$13.4M**

Source: WBUR Edify, October 2016, http://www.wbur.org/edify/2016/10/27/where-the-money-comes-from-in-the-fight-over-charter-schools

Insiders with the Massachusetts branch of FES also note that the "Yes" side was so disorganized it failed to highlight the hypocrisy inherent to the "No" campaign. "We should have been asking questions like 'where do union leaders send their children to school?'" one "Yes" campaigner pointed out.[19]

Charter detractors knew that they benefited from dissention and disorder in the ranks of "Yes on 2" supporters. In 2017, Barbara Madeloni, President of the Massachusetts Teachers Association, issued a statement of thanks to the "Yes" campaign for bringing the question to the ballot. Implicit in Madeloni's "thank you" was an acknowledgement that "Yes on 2" had failed at its own game. The "No" side had been confident it would win from the beginning.[20]

Another important influence on the campaign was that which was missing. Comparatively few of the Commonwealth's most prominent supporters of charter schools lent a loud voice to the "Yes" campaign. Charter school operators and leaders in Massachusetts have fought long and hard to exist, and many were loathe to risk the charter school seats that they have won or the alliances they have formed unless there was a clear path to victory. Too many did not see that path via the ballot box.

Were charter school leaders right? It seems they were. In the end, the vote against Question 2 was overwhelming. Of the handful of towns where the majority voted "Yes," most were white, wealthy suburbs. This outcome was counter to the assumption of charter advocates that families that benefit from charter schools — those in places like Boston, Springfield, Lawrence, and Lowell — would want more of these schools. They made this assumption because in these communities outcomes are strong and waitlists are long.

As the previous analysis notes, there are a variety of reasons why the ballot measure didn't pass and no one factor was an identifiable tipping point. However, the campaign to expand charter school options via the ballot box isn't the only reason why so many voters — even those who benefit from charters — were inclined to say "No on 2." A less-discussed explanation for the outcome of Question 2 is how evolving charter school policies have shaped perceptions of charter schools in the Commonwealth more generally.

The Status Quo of the Charter Sector

For years, reform-minded Massachusetts charter school advocates have touted the accomplishments of the Commonwealth's charter schools, but they haven't always acted in the best interests of the charter movement. Specifically, they have not pushed the Legislature or BESE to create a policy environment that allows charters to fulfill the various purposes they were meant to serve under the MERA. Instead, charter school advocates have maintained a narrow focus on the academic outcomes that charter schools achieve, pointing to gold standard research that touts the success of Boston's charter sector in particular.

The academic accomplishments of charters are real and worthy of examination and praise (they comprise the first half of this book!). However, a failure to look at what charters currently are in relation to what they were meant to be has led to a myopic view of the movement's success — one the public may not tolerate for much longer.

Especially during the lead-up to Question 2, reformers failed to realize that Massachusetts charters have come to have a very distinct reputation, one that can elicit negative sentiment even among some of the most common consumers of charters. The reputation Boston's charters have is one of sameness: a no-excuses approach to education that is increasingly characterized as inflexible and sometimes out of touch with the needs of today's students. It is also increasingly — though not always fairly — associated with high suspension rates and disciplinary policies that are punitive as opposed to educative.[21]

There are several important things to note about the no-excuses approach to education and the attention it has received. First, not every successful charter is or has been of the no excuses variety. Many of the Commonwealth's most successful charters at one time adopted or were given this moniker, while others have never associated their pedagogy with a no-excuses approach.

NO EXCUSES

The term "no excuses" came to be associated with a variety of different charter schools in the early 2000s. Perhaps the most well known organization to model the "no-excuses" approach is the Knowledge is Power Program (KIPP). "No-excuses" schools have most or all of the following features:

(1) high behavioral and academic expectations for all students;

(2) strict behavioral and disciplinary codes;

(3) a college preparatory curriculum for all;

(4) expanded learning time; and

(5) rigorous teacher training, assessment, and feedback programs and policies.

Second, at the start of the state's charter movement in the 1990s, no-excuses schools were a welcome and heralded innovation. They provided the rigor, structure, and high expectations that too many district schools did not. They also extended the school day and year, cultivated their own faculty, and committed to things like personalized tutoring for every student, when district schools could not. Most importantly, they consistently communicated one overarching message: They would work relentlessly to provide all students with the education they deserve; they refused to accept any excuse that adults might provide when they fail to help students achieve, including the excuse of poverty.[22]

When the Massachusetts charter movement developed in the 1990s, this message was novel. Since the 1960s, and into the era of desegregating schools, families had been told that poverty caused underachievement. Family background, schools implicitly and explicitly communicated to students, was the main determinant of whether a student would graduate from high school and go on to college. In the early 1990s, sociologists Herrnstein and Murray received a great deal of attention for their book *The Bell Curve*, which argued that the black-white achievement gap was a function of innate intelligence, rather than socioeconomic status or systemic inequality.[23] Though the academic community easily refuted the validity of this baseless argument, the book captured the popular imagination.

No-excuses schools were important and innovative because they turned this and other narratives about academic achievement on their heads. They acknowledged that the responsibility for educating children lay with the school as an institution. They framed underachievement as a failure of the system, rather than the family or the person. They committed to doing "whatever it takes" to provide every child equal access to a high-quality education. They also taught students to operate within rigid systems and structures, utilizing dress codes and demerit systems, and emphasizing soft skills, such as public speaking, that would enable students to navigate the adult world.[24]

"The traditional school my son was in wasn't working for us. I applied to 3 or 4 charter schools, and people told me it was 'a shot in hell' to get in. KIPP was the only charter school that we heard back from. From the beginning, it has been a good fit for my son. My son is autistic and, right now, he is not an independent thinker. He needs structure and guidance to understand how things work, and the school and his teachers are providing that for him."
– Charter school parent of a KIPP, Boston third-grade student

In 2017, many parents still appreciate and seek the structure offered by schools once associated with a no-excuses approach. They also continue to appreciate the message that "demography is not destiny." At the same time, some question the methods associated with this approach. They wonder how such rigid structures will help students navigate the comparatively unstructured world of college. They worry that the model makes certain assumptions about low-income urban students, such as that they won't know how to dress "professionally" unless the school teaches them or that they need rigid rules and discipline to succeed academically.

As a result, charters are clearly moving to disassociate themselves with the no-excuses label. Of those schools that have been called no excuses in the past, many have made intentional attempts to evolve their approaches, integrating aspects of the model that serve kids well (such as high expectations and rigorous curricula) with new pedagogies better aligned to the academic and socioemotional needs of individual students and families. A 2015 study of diversity in major charter sectors found that only two urban charter schools in Massachusetts were identified as taking a no-excuses approach.[25] A more in-depth 2013 study, however, found that at least two-thirds of urban charter schools in Massachusetts identified with some or all of the features of the no-excuses pedagogy.[26]

But it takes longer to shift public perception than it does to change a label on a website, and angst about the relationship of charters to the no-excuses approach was at the forefront of many conversations about charter schools in the lead-up to the 2016 ballot initiative. The opposition succeeded at casting the methods charter schools use to achieve strong academic outcomes in a negative light. They suggested that charters would not be successful if not for rigid disciplinary policies that effectively weed out low-performing students. These arguments are refuted by data presented in chapters 2 and 3 of this book, but they nonetheless won favor with some of the public.

Of course, the popularity (or lack thereof) of one pedagogical approach is not solely responsible for the public's perception of charter schools. Where some see dated practice or a lack of innovation in the sector, others see opportunity to replicate a proven model. Some of the most successful charter schools have a lot in common, and these commonalities are important for understanding strong teaching and learning.

Massachusetts charter schools tend to do things identified in the research as "best practices" for boosting academic achievement: They extend the school day and year and personalize learning by using one-to-one tutoring. They also develop their own teachers and teacher pipelines in specific and often innovative ways. Indeed, some of the best charter schools, as discussed earlier in this book, pioneered an approach to data-driven instruction that is now used in schools throughout the country.[27] But when common practices become sameness, schools become less flexible and, in some cases, less able to adapt to the needs of individuals or even specific student populations. Where innovation once existed, a new status quo takes hold, and families are left with fewer and fewer distinct educational options. The new status quo for the Massachusetts charter school movement can be traced back to 2010, when the Legislature raised the cap on charter schools for the fourth time since passage of the MERA.

Compromise and the Cap Raise

In 2010, the Obama administration provided charter advocates across the country with an unforeseen opportunity. Under *Race to the Top,* states that prioritized the expansion of charter schools received preference for federal grants. For the first time since the Massachusetts charter school law was conceived, charter supporters and detractors came together to win additional funding for the state's public schools.

As part of legislation entitled *An Achievement Gap Act,* the Commonwealth raised the cap on charter schools in the lowest-performing 10 percent of districts. This became known as the "smart cap"— a way to make more charter seats available in districts where demand was highest, without raising the overall cap.[28]

There were two main components to the smart cap. First, the cap would only be raised in the lowest-performing 10 percent of Massachusetts districts, which would see the limit on charter school spending raised from 9 percent to 18 percent of net school spending. Second, new charters in districts subject to the increase would only be awarded to "proven providers," or charter operators with a track record of meeting a high bar for both helping students achieve and sound school governance. A state and one city in particular (Boston), which was starved for more charter school seats, viewed the legislation as a boon to the movement.

And if "boon" translates to immediate growth, charter advocates were right. After years of approving few if any new charter seats in Boston, in 2010–11 the Commonwealth authorized 16 new charter schools, all operated by groups with proven performance records. The thirst for more charter schools was so fierce among both families and charter operators that the state called a moratorium on new charters in some districts, like Boston, in the 2011–12 cycle so as not to immediately give away every newly available seat.

But more charters in charter-starved cities came with trade-offs. By only awarding seats to "proven providers," the Common-

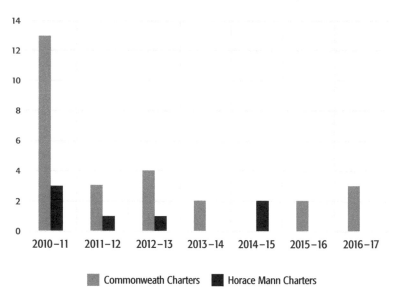

Massachusetts Charter Schools Authorized, 2010–2017

Commonweath Charters   Horace Mann Charters

wealth was not only limiting charter opportunities to a handful of operators, it was foreclosing innovation. Even though DESE would have some freedom to interpret who was and was not a proven provider, the legislation made clear that new charter seats would only be awarded to people and organizations who had previously operated academically successful schools.[29]

For DESE, MCAS scores are a central measure of academic success, and the providers that it immediately authorized in 2010 — Match Charter Public School, KIPP, The Community Group and others — were all known high performers.[30] The awarding of new seats to these organizations was not a bad thing; many more children have access to high-quality education because these organizations expanded. However, it's impossible to know what new, high-quality opportunities might exist today had the 2010 legislation not placed a constraint on who can serve students.

The legislation further shaped the charter movement by

implicitly labeling the type of community and student that charters should serve. By limiting meaningful charter growth to only the lowest-performing districts and doing nothing to incent charter growth in communities that hadn't yet reached the cap, the legislation paints charter schools as an alternative to struggling districts, places where lucky lottery winners can have a chance at a better education. Whereas the first crop of Massachusetts charter schools included a variety of school types that served students from diverse racial, cultural, and socioeconomic backgrounds, charters were now understood to exist solely for poor, minority students looking for a "way out" of districts.[31]

The 2010 legislation also included language that has enabled DESE to pile new regulations on charter schools. In many cases, those regulations do little to improve the educational experience for students while curtailing charter school autonomy and forcing charter operators to focus on compliance.

But some of the regulations instituted in 2010 were, in hindsight, sensible. One is a requirement that charter schools "backfill" (or continue to admit students) certain grades until halfway through the school year when they have available seats. In 2010, there was fear that a mandate to backfill could inhibit a school's ability to create a cohesive culture, but few Massachusetts charter operators have reported that backfilling is a problem, and many were doing it already. Moreover, backfilling puts charters and districts on a more even playing field in terms of student mobility and enrollment; districts have no choice but to accept students when they arrive, no matter what time of year.

The second sensible set of regulations was meant to ensure that charters serve proportionate numbers of students with special needs. In exchange for district schools providing student addresses so charters can more effectively recruit all students (something that districts were loathe to do), charters were required to develop "recruitment and retention" plans to demonstrate to DESE that they are working to serve special populations.

While the intent of these regulations was to ensure greater

access and equity in the charter sector, they have not always been well implemented by the state. Most charter operators note that having student contact information has made a big difference in attracting a more diverse student body. The recruitment and retention plans that charter operators have to file, on the other hand, have resulted in additional time spent on paperwork and compliance, and there is little evidence that they are effective.

Instead of simply measuring outcomes (has the number of special education students that charters are serving increased?) DESE has ensured that charters are doing a lot of unnecessary work on the front end, describing *how they intend* to accomplish something, instead of whether something of value has been accomplished. But a little more paperwork for charter school leaders pales in comparison to how the state has redefined who gets access to charter schools and who does not.

Regulating Access to the Charter Sector

Following the 2010 cap lift and in the midst of *Race to the Top*, charter advocates were hopeful that the Legislature would acknowledge both the demand for and impact of charters by raising the cap again, this time with fewer strings attached. In 2014, the state Senate rejected a House-approved bill that would have raised the statewide charter school cap. The same year, BESE changed the way the smart cap would be implemented by rejiggering the formula for determining which districts are in the bottom 10 percent.[32]

From 2010 to 2015, the lowest-performing districts in the state were identified based on student achievement results alone. In June 2014, the commissioner of DESE proposed and the BESE approved a new formula that takes into account both overall student achievement (75 percent) and the amount of growth students in a district have achieved (25 percent).[33] The rationale for the change was that the Commonwealth should provide incentives for districts to help students grow and that student growth should be rewarded. Overall test scores, especially in large districts, sometimes mask student achievement gains, and this was part of the reason for including a separate growth measure. BESE saw student growth as a main reason for the *Achievement Gap Act* of 2010, and was motivated to incorporate it as part of the state's overall accountability formula.

Then-BESE vice-chair Harneen Chernow noted in 2014[34]:

> Looking at the data, I saw that achievement on MCAS corresponds absolutely with the socio-economic status of a district... But when we looked at the data around growth, and where the greatest growth was, we saw a very different picture. From my perspective, a goal of the state's accountability system is growth — we are evaluating teachers based on growth, so why aren't we incorporating that into district accountability determinations as well? We are looking at where there is improvement and innovation and change and where districts are responding to need by doing good things. Our goal should be to support and reinforce these outcomes. This was the whole accountability piece — (the formula) was not just about determining the bottom 10 percent. The goal was to have one streamlined accountability system that was more transparent for schools, and parents and everyone to understand...

This rationale, as explained by Chernow at the time, seems reasonable. But as with all things related to charter politics in the Commonwealth, revamping the state's accountability formula had predictable ramifications on the growth of the charter movement.

Then-Commissioner of Education Mitchell Chester warned BESE of the ramifications of using growth as a factor in the formula when he explained that overemphasizing growth in student achievement — as opposed to looking at absolute overall student achievement in a district — would "start to distort the identification of schools and districts most in need of our assistance."[35] He did not believe that student achievement growth should account for more than 25 percent of a district's overall accountability rating.

Chester knew that persistently struggling districts would be more able to show significant growth, because it is much easier to bring up the very lowest test scores than it is to bring below-average scores up to an acceptable level. Just because student achievement improves does not mean that a district is serving all students well. He also understood that some of the state's largest urban districts, where demand for charter schools is high, would be in a position to exit the lowest-performing 10 percent of districts if growth were heavily weighted.

Charter supporters saw the move to include growth as a factor as a example of hostility to charters on BESE's part. Then-Governor Deval Patrick was at times a critic and at other times (in the lead-up to *Race to the Top*) a tepid supporter of charter schools, and BESE was composed mainly of Patrick appointees. Charter supporters perceived that many board members were hostile to the movement. Some viewed the revised accountability formula as one more mechanism to stall charter school expansion.[36]

And the formula for determining growth is tricky, even unreliable, according to some psychometricians. In the context of Massachusetts, consider two grade 8 students in 2014. Both scored 254 on the grade 6 ELA test and 250 on the grade 8 ELA test. The first student, however, scored 240 on the grade 7 ELA test and the second student scored 262 on the grade 7 ELA test. The first student has a 2014 Student Growth Percentile (SGP) of 78 and the second student has a 2014 SGP of 3. Both students were proficient on MCAS all three years, but the second year difference creates a tremendous SGP difference. In reality, it is hard to see how these two students have such different "growth."[37]

Regardless of the formula's reliability, the Commonwealth began using it in the 2015 application cycle. Based on overall student achievement and growth, DESE determined that year, for the first time, which communities would be "in" and "out" of the bottom 10 percent and therefore which communities would qualify for additional charter school seats.

Since 2014, low-performing districts like Fall River have fallen out of the bottom 10 percent, despite continuing to fail large numbers of students. In 2016, for example, 27 percent and 25 percent of Fall River's students scored in the "warning/ failing" category on the math and science MCAS tests, respectively. But that year Fall River was not in the bottom 10 percent mainly because student growth accounts for 25 percent of the formula. Overall, its students did not perform much better on MCAS than a place like Boston, which has remained in the bottom 10 percent.[38]

In another example, students in Lawrence have shown enough growth in some years to take the district out of the bottom 10 percent only to show less growth in subsequent years and fall in again. This demonstrates that the state's new formula can be volatile. In Lawrence's case, this volatility doesn't help matters; the district has made great strides in recent years in part by leveraging charter providers, creating new charter/district partnerships, and adopting many practices that were first scaled in the charter sector, such as one-to-one tutoring for struggling students.[39]

And the addition of growth scores to the formula that determines which communities see an increase in the charter cap is the reason these improving but still struggling communities may not be able to leverage charter schools in the future. Because communities like Boston see charters as one very strong form of high-quality education for students, the formula spurs an almost perverse desire that Boston not improve too much; there is nervousness that student growth will be so high as to push the district out of the bottom 10 percent and foreclose the possibility of even a few additional charter school seats.[40] On the other hand, some communities that have now fallen into the bottom 10 percent have no strong history with charter schools, and the community expresses little desire to welcome charter operators.

But whether communities should even want to use charter schools as one mechanism for improving public education is not the point. In Massachusetts, policymakers determine who gets access to a charter school education and who doesn't. *This fundamentally undermines the intent of the charter school law, which was in part to provide families with more options.* Those who wrote the law were not reserving charter schools and their promise for certain types of families and communities, nor were they forcing charter schools on others. Instead, they were promoting the idea that educational choice matters; they believed that all families, regardless of social background, can and should be allowed to make good choices for their children.

And in curtailing choice for families — especially those who don't have the means to pay for private schools — the Commonwealth is also driving away prospective charter operators.

With little room to establish schools in the communities where they are wanted and little ability to implement new concepts under the proven provider clause, would-be education innovators and entrepreneurs are taking their ideas elsewhere. They are going to places like New York and California, where the charter laws are more flexible and charter caps — where they exist at all — are more reasonable.

Even successful charter school networks — groups of charters run by a central entity and often based on a particular educational philosophy and/or pedagogical approach — see no opportunity in Massachusetts. The nation's most ubiquitous and successful charter provider, KIPP, has two schools in the Commonwealth and no plans to apply for more seats where they don't exist. Other highly successful networks like Achievement First have not even applied for seats in Massachusetts, despite operating schools in New York, Connecticut, and Rhode Island. One of the fastest-growing and most innovative new networks in the country, Rocketship, won't bother to apply either, seeing little room to make an impact in the state, given its stringent cap on charter growth.[41]

By encouraging innovators to leave and doing nothing to attract new talent, the policy environment in Massachusetts has created a "brain drain" in the state's education sector. This diversion of talent to other places has tangible consequences for a state that incubated some of the best charter schools founded by some of the nation's brightest young education reformers.[42]

Whereas other states used to look at Massachusetts as a model for how to grow strong charter schools, the state is now looking outside its borders and watching as other states experiment and succeed with innovative new school models. The Commonwealth's policy environment is halting the growth of an important movement and stripping families of the right to choose the education they desire for their children; something states looking to build strong charter laws and sectors should avoid.

CHAPTER 7

Lessons Learned:

Charter School Policy and the Massachusetts Experience

W HEN CHARTER SCHOOLS WERE CONCEIVED in the late 1980s, it was thought that they could be laboratories for innovation and that lessons learned from charter schools could inform meaningful change in districts. While districts have adopted some charter school innovations, on balance there has been more hostility and competition between charters and districts than sharing of ideas and goodwill.

Likewise, a look at the diversity of charter school laws and policies around the country shows that states haven't learned nearly enough from one another. Charter watchers know that some policies foster charter school quality while others are a hindrance. Different factions of the national education reform establishment agree that, at minimum, laws should provide charters real autonomy in exchange for rigorous accountability if quality schools are to exist. Authorizer type and diversity are also key ingredients that impact charter school quality.

Massachusetts receives high marks for granting its schools real autonomy and holding them strictly accountable for outcomes. But its single authorizer is a bureaucracy that oversees all public schools, and this flies in the face of best practice (even if the authorizer is strong). The charter school cap and the proven provider clause are other parts of the charter school law that national advocates, who perceive them as roadblocks to growth and innovation, would like to see changed.

Even considering these roadblocks, the academic track record of Massachusetts's charters is unparalleled. This presents a conundrum for some policy experts. How can Boston's charters in particular be so great, when the state's charter school law rates only slightly above average in comparison to others? Some see the Commonwealth, with its high-performing district schools, university culture, and strong teacher and school leader pipelines as an exception to the rule. Others wonder how much better Massachusetts charters could be if state policies were changed.

There are a number of important lessons other states can learn from Massachusetts. Many of these include policies and practices worthy of emulation. Others are examples of what not to do. The latter illustrate unintended consequences of otherwise well-intentioned policy decisions.

LESSON 1:

Charter schools are a critical component of any education reform agenda, but charter diversity and access to charters matter.

Charter schools were but one component of an overall Massachusetts education reform agenda that included a revised approach to school funding, a common understanding of what students should know and be able to do, and a structure that holds all schools accountable for outcomes. Charter schools were the only component of that agenda that put power in the hands of parents and created space for new ideas about the structure, content, and delivery of education — both academic and non-academic — to flourish.

When given the option to try charter public schools, parents took it. Those who were dissatisfied with the status quo in their neighborhoods saw charter schools not just as a way out of a failing district but as an opportunity to experience a new approach to schooling. Sometimes the new approach was about curriculum and pedagogy, other times it was about a different school culture, or reimagining relationships between teachers and students and even schools and families.

Charter schools, especially in the early days of the charter movement, were an innovative option for families. They were not district schools by another name because Commonwealth charters were completely independent of their district counterparts. *Policymakers should not underestimate the relationship between charter school independence and charter quality.*

Moreover, at the beginning of the movement, Massachusetts had a vested interest in allowing some degree of experimentation. This diversity within the charter sector provided another form of real choice for families. Once it had established its commitment to closing schools that did not meet expectations, the Commonwealth took some chances on new approaches to schooling, even under the charter cap.

In large part because the Legislature designed charters to be their own districts, and because real choice and diversity existed among charters early on, hundreds of thousands of Massachusetts families have benefited from charter schools.[1]

Unfortunately, tens of thousands of families have tried but failed to reap the benefits of charters. These are the families who have not been chosen in charter lotteries and families who have been deprived of true school choice because there is little room for expansion under the charter school cap and little room for innovation under current charter school policy. In the 2017–18 school year, there were 27,416 unique students on charter school waiting lists. This number counts only unique students, not those who have entered more than one lottery.[2] Charters will continue to benefit some who want them, but the Commonwealth must revise its policies if all families are to have equal access to charter school choices.

LESSON 2:

Real autonomy leads to real quality in the charter sector.

In Massachusetts, charter school autonomy is real for two reasons. First, the Legislature granted Commonwealth charters very specific freedoms; in particular, the freedom to galvanize around a specific theme or mission, set school budgets, and determine the length of the school day and year. These freedoms have allowed charters to innovate in various ways.

Second, by allowing charters to operate as their own school districts, the Legislature also ensured that they would not have to be part of the local collective bargaining unit (teachers' union). This gave charter school leaders the autonomy to assemble their own staffs and dismiss ineffective teachers without costly processes that take resources away from students. It also allows them to set their own salaries. Studies show a relationship between attending a school where teachers don't engage in collective bargaining and better employment opportunities and higher earning potential for students later in life.[3]

Other studies make clear that charter school autonomy, more generally, is related to better academic outcomes.[4] Some of the most successful schools, such as those discussed in chapter 4 of this book, are successful because they provide extra learning time by extending school days and years. The same schools assemble budgets that prioritize students rather than adults, and many of them have developed sophisticated talent recruitment pipelines and teacher training programs. It is difficult to do these things in district settings because of long, detailed collective bargaining agreements that prescribe a teacher's work day down to the minute, often reducing working hours compared to non-union school environments.[5] Charters, on the other hand, can be nimble.

Autonomy alone is not sufficient for producing excellent charter schools, but the highest performing schools in the country view autonomy as necessary to their success.[6] States that design charter school policies devoid of real autonomy are, in most cases, creating district schools by another name.

> "The autonomy that I have, as a school leader, matters. When it comes to hiring, I can look for a fit betweeninstitutional ideals and vision and a candidate's ideals and vision. The autonomy to assemble my own staff is critical."
> – Charter school leader, Western Massachusetts

LESSON 3:

Real accountability leads to real quality, but an emphasis on the wrong type of accountability can lead to regulatory creep and an overreliance on unreliable data.

From the beginning, the Commonwealth has been unafraid to close charter schools that don't serve students well. But it takes more than just a willingness to close failing schools for accountability to work. Massachusetts charter schools have always been held to clear performance standards, academic and otherwise, and this matters.[7]

All public schools are accountable for results, but charters are subject to renewal every five years and can be closed if they fail to meet expectations. The Commonwealth's charter renewal process is designed to gather both quantitative and qualitative information about charter school performance, and the commissioner and the Board of Elementary and Secondary Education look specifically for evidence that a school has been faithful to its charter, academically successful, and operates in a way that promotes the organization's viability.[8] The renewal process is detailed. When it works, it functions not only as an audit of the school's performance but also as a tool for school leaders and faculty to reflect on their performance and constantly improve.

The Charter School Renewal Cycle*

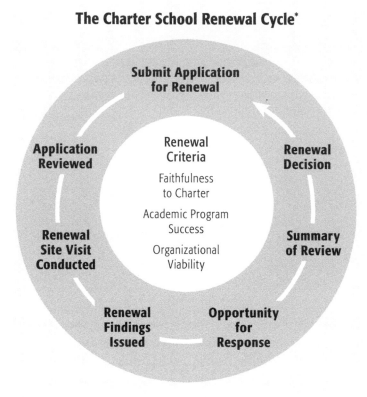

The state has rigorous tools for measuring whether schools are meeting expectations. MCAS (and now Next-Generation MCAS) has been one tool for measuring academic success. Audits of schools' financial records and other documents help ensure that each school and board is operating in a financially responsible way. Site visits and in-depth interviews with school staff help the Commonwealth understand the extent to which a school is fulfilling the terms of its charter, especially with regard to curricula and programming.[9]

And over time, the state has developed additional require-

---

* Massachusetts Department of Education, Charter School Renewal Inspection Protocol, June 2017.

ments and metrics for determining charter school quality. Enrollment records can help the state assess whether the school provides access to diverse groups of students. Tracking dropout, graduation, and student attrition rates can help state education officials understand whether the school strives to enable all students to achieve academic success.

Importantly, the data the Commonwealth collects and uses for the renewal process are public and published annually. This allows all public schools — districts, charter, and others — to understand how they perform in context. This transparency also empowers parents and the general public to understand major aspects of school quality.[10]

While other public schools may be closed when they underperform (another lesson taken from charter school policy and applied to districts), closure is rare and the process onerous. *Charters, on the other hand, are conceived and exist under a threat of closure.* There is a process to close a charter school, starting with providing warnings and assistance and ending with a BESE vote to revoke a charter.

This rigorous accountability cycle, coupled with the autonomy charter schools have, is one of the main reasons for excellence in the Massachusetts charter sector. In states where poor schools are allowed to persist, the threat of closure is toothless and is not perceived to be real. In states where charter closures are arbitrary or based only on one measure of success, schools that benefit students are closed before they can benefit more. These things don't usually happen under the Massachusetts system.

But this evolving accountability system isn't perfect. Regulatory creep, described in Chapter 6 as the increase in compliance-based paperwork, is one trade-off. The renewal process takes time and human capital. It has also become more onerous over time.

Most charters are continuously focused on some aspect of their renewal process; they are constantly collecting and documenting relevant data and producing paperwork to comply with state expectations.[11] In this respect, charters now behave

MASSACHUSETTS CHARTERS ARE HIGHLY ACCOUNTABLE:

Of the 112 charters that it has granted to date, the Commonwealth has revoked 5 charters and opted not to renew 2 schools. Ten schools have surrendered their charters after opening.[*]

more like districts than ever before. As the accountability process becomes more detailed and charters are accountable for additional outcomes, they begin to behave more and more like districts. There are measures the state could take to streamline accountability processes.

If regulatory creep is one risk of the state's current accountability system, the high premium the state places on test data is another. Although test scores raise the profile of many charters, policymakers learned in the era of *No Child Left Behind* that when test scores are overemphasized, schools are compelled to focus instruction on what is tested to the exclusion of other things.

On one hand, standardized tests are an important tool that should not be dismissed; using MCAS to determine whether some schools are drastically underserving students has revealed inequities among public schools and forced state intervention in cases of egregious underachievement. Were it not for strong MCAS results, many charters would not have the stellar reputations that they do today.

On the other hand, such a strong emphasis on test scores as an indicator of success has encouraged some schools to over rely on a sometimes unreliable measure of what students know. Policymakers and psychometricians understand that standardized tests are a better indicator of how students perform in comparison to their peers, or how they have grown over time. Tests are not really reliable measures of what students know and can do within or between subjects.[12] As charters with stellar test

---

[*] Massachusetts Department of Elementary and Secondary Education, Charter School Fact Sheet

Learning from Massachusetts

(1) Ensure that charters options are diverse and accessible to all students.

(2) Provide charters real autonomy to do something different.

(3) Hold charters accountable for outcomes, not compliance.

(4) Consider multiple, high-quality authorizers.

(5) Vanquish charter school caps.

(6) Make funding for all schools equitable and transparent.

(7) Purposefully design policies to foster excellence, diversity, and innovation.

(8) Consider the political mechanisms that will establish and maintain a successful charter sector.

scores struggle to help students persist in college, the limits of test-based accountability are becoming increasingly apparent.[13]

The same holds for other aspects of the accountability system. Massachusetts charters focus mainly on the issues the Commonwealth values because the next charter renewal is always on the horizon. In 2010, the state said "enroll more ELL students," and charters focused mightily on doing so. More recently, the state has said "reduce out-of-school suspensions," and charters have begun to eliminate discipline protocols that use suspension as a tool, sometimes without providing strong alternatives.

These are not bad things. All schools should serve students that want access to their services. All providers should consider the many disciplinary tools they have at their disposal and choose those that are going to help students stay in school and be productive members of the school community. However, in haste to comply with the Commonwealth, some schools might fail to thoughtfully undertake and implement new initiatives. In the context of changing disciplinary procedures, a school might risk destroying a school culture in which students feel safe in favor of reducing suspensions at any cost.

LESSON 4:

A rigorous single authorizer can produce high-quality charters, but it may do so at the expense of autonomy and innovation.

Most national charter advocates and advocacy organizations believe multiple authorizers lead to a more robust, diverse, and effective charter sector. The National Association of Charter School Authorizers notes that "the presence of multiple authorizers can strengthen a state's charter school sector because a diversity of authorizers can promote professional practices among authorizers and provide checks and balances in charter approval, oversight and renewal decisions."[14]

Moreover, states that allow only one authorizer, especially if that authorizer is a local school district (or school board), tend to have fewer charter schools and existing schools tend to have less autonomy.[15] A 2013 survey conducted by the Center for Education Reform found that states with strong, multiple chartering authorities have almost three-and-a-half times more charter schools than states that only allow local board approval.[16]

While Massachusetts does not allow districts to authorize Commonwealth charters (though districts do play a role in reauthorizing Horace Mann charter schools), its single authorizer model, coupled with the charter school cap, is one clear reason why Massachusetts has so few charter schools. And because the sole authorizer is the same state bureaucracy that oversees all public schools, conflict of interest questions arise. The Commonwealth might feel pressured to limit charter school growth to appease its other constituents, such as districts and the teachers' unions that are associated with them.

And when there is only one authorizer in a state, there are fewer voices to advocate for best practices, and a greater chance that politics will take hold. In 2013, when BESE changed the formula for determining which districts would be subject to an increase in the charter school cap, then-Commissioner of Education Mitchell Chester was vocal in his concern that growth not be too prevalent a factor — but ultimately compelled to work with the state board, which would make the decision.[17] Were another authorizer present, there may have been more robust debate about the consequences of a growth-model formula.

It is also notable that the growth in compliance-oriented regulation that charters experience corresponds with moving the charter school office out of an independent authorizing office (the Secretariat) and into DESE.[18] The department could choose to protect charters from regulatory creep and ensure their autonomy, but it has not.

One of the reasons for treating charters like all other schools with regard to regulation might be the department's lack of dedicated charter resources. While the Charter School Office was small even under the earlier education secretariat, under DESE's structure some of the few people working with and for charter schools might also be overseeing district schools. This is not to suggest that the department has no charter school advocates, but there is a real sense that DESE cannot vocally advocate for charters.

Perhaps the biggest hazard of the single authorizer model is the risk aversion it, coupled with the charter cap, breeds. With no collaborative partner, no one else in the Commonwealth to look to for strong and/or innovative authorizing practices, DESE and BESE have become more and more comfortable authorizing "tried and true" school models. In states with multiple authorizers, different types of authorizers can leverage expertise and dedicate useful resources to authorization processes.

Universities, for example, might be adept at authorizing schools that experiment with various pedagogical models. Independent charter school boards can bring an advocate's perspective to authorization processes. They are also not beholden to the critique that they exist to serve all public schools. While Massachusetts's sole authorizer has done an excellent job of focusing on charter quality vis-à-vis academic outcomes, it is compelling to consider how the sector might look if the Commonwealth's only authorizer had one or more peers.

LESSON 5:
Charter caps can lead to thoughtful authorizing. They can also foreclose opportunity.

It is difficult to look at the history of charter schooling in Massachusetts and not attribute the quality of the state's charter sector, in some ways, to the cap. Former Secretary of Education Michael Sentance acknowledged that in the early days of the charter movement, when the state had few successful authorizing models to look to, the charter cap forced his team to make difficult decisions about which charter school proposals were likely to yield the best academic experiences and outcomes for students.[19] As demand for charter schools outpaced the number of seats available under the cap, pressure to distinguish between "winning" and "losing" charter school models only grew. With so many families, especially in urban centers, demanding a higher quality of education, why wouldn't the state give those families a sure bet?

Taking a chance on unproven new models, no matter how innovative or promising they may have seemed, came with other risks. It is much more costly and time consuming for the state to close a school that isn't working than to take a chance on a new school that looks something like other schools that have succeeded.[20] Thus the cap that played a small role in picking one of the nation's best charter sectors (Boston) has played a very prominent role in that sector's inability to grow. It has also contributed to that sector's inability to diversify and satisfy the shifting educational needs and expectations of a new generation of students and families.

The cap has harmed the charter sector in an even more insidious way: It has bred some of the most divisive charter politics in the nation. The charter v. district debate in Massachusetts is predicated on the cap and inflamed when raising it is proposed.

Were the cap itself not a question, the Commonwealth could better focus on an authorizing strategy that emphasizes quality and innovation. Instead of debating "yes or no" on a cap lift, charter advocates and detractors might instead focus on the more meaningful questions that should drive any education reform debate. Questions such as "What does the Commonwealth need to do to provide access to excellent schools — public or charter — for all students?" "What types of schools will help different types of students meet their full potential?" and "How can we reconceive our school funding system to ensure equity and access, no matter what school a child attends?"

LESSON 6:

Funding makes a difference, and so do perceptions about how funding works.

As outlined in chapter 5, Massachusetts deserves high marks for how it funds charter schools. From the beginning, it has ensured that students who attend charter schools receive the same per-pupil funding as their district counterparts. By starting with the principle that funding should follow the student, the Legislature made the bold assertion that education dollars belong to families, not schools or district bureaucracies. This counters the assumption implicit in some arguments against school choice that public money designated for education should flow to institutions instead of families.

In designing a charter school funding system that requires districts to send tuition to the charter schools students attend, the Commonwealth accomplishes two worthy objectives. First, it ensures that families and students are accessing (though indirectly) the local property tax base that all families pay into for education. Second, it protects charter schools from becoming

147

line items in state budgets, vulnerable to cuts that other public schools might not experience because of the multiple sources from which they can draw funds.

Other states would do well to emulate these Massachusetts charter school funding principles, with caveats. Per-pupil allocation is only one component of charter school funding, and Massachusetts charter schools still receive minimal assistance in the areas of facilities and maintenance.[21] Whether schools adjust school budgets or raise philanthropic money to cover these costs, they are monies that could otherwise be spent on students and teachers. This puts charters on uneven financial footing compared to districts.

Additionally, charter schools receive a general allocation meant to cover the higher costs of educating students with special needs, but that allocation is not tied to the enrollment of that student population. As a result, charters that enroll low numbers of students with special educational needs may receive more state funding than they need — funding that could be used in the sending district. On the other hand, when charter schools enroll high numbers of special needs students (and an increasing number of charter schools do), they may not have sufficient resources to adequately serve them. Were per-pupil allocations more closely tied to actual enrollment and student characteristics, both districts and charters would be better served.[22]

Perhaps the most interesting aspect of charter school funding in Massachusetts is the reimbursement formula the Commonwealth enacted the first time it lifted the charter cap. Massachusetts is unique in the nation for reimbursing districts for six years when they lose students to charters. These reimbursements (when the state fully funds them) enable districts to adjust to shifts in enrollment that could otherwise harm overall operating budgets. But they are also very costly to taxpayers and, as some national charter advocates have argued, prevent districts from learning to be nimble and to right-size their operations. Part of the problem is that district budgets are often large and not very transparent. It can be difficult to determine whether and how declining enrollment is negatively impacting districts or if districts simply need to manage their finances more transparently and efficiently.

Despite generous district reimbursements, charter school opponents still successfully paint charters as a financial drain on districts. This speaks to one of the most important lessons Massachusetts can provide to other states: Perception matters. In part because school funding (not just charter school funding) in the Commonwealth is so opaque, it is easy for districts and charters alike to claim they are not equitably funded, no matter the reality. When districts lose students to charters and have to send tuition payments to the schools, they feel a real loss of funds. Likewise, when charters have to decide between providing students with services and paying rent on a building, they feel a real financial burden. But most importantly, when families who do not have access to charter schools or choose not to use charter schools perceive that money that could be spent on their children is going "out of district," they perceive an inequity that is very personal in nature.

Clarity and transparency in school funding could make a real difference in Massachusetts and other states. Designing a system that funds students and families rather than institutions can also begin to shift perceptions about how we consume education in the United States.

LESSON 7:

*Excellence, diversity, and innovation can coexist,
if policies are purposefully designed.*

Excellence clearly exists in the Massachusetts charter sector. Innovation is also present, but there is less room for new innovations under the charter school cap. And while it would be a mischaracterization to say there is no diversity in the charter sector, it is true that there was greater diversity at the beginning of the movement than there has been in the last decade.

In the beginning of the movement, before the cap limited charter growth, the state authorized charter schools in various parts of the Commonwealth. There tended to be greater diversity, especially in terms of pedagogical approach, in the suburbs. As the cap encroached, the state became more and more risk averse, awarding charters to organizations that were proposing proven methods and avoiding those that might have been new and promising, but were unproven.

This kind of reaction from authorizers is common, and even understandable. When charter opportunities are limited, and especially when those most likely to take advantage of charters are students who are perceived to have few quality educational options, authorizers become less willing to bet on innovation and gamble with a child's education.[23] This is an unfortunate consequence of bad circumstances coupled with good intentions. Who is to say that some typical charter school consumers wouldn't prize innovative school opportunities over the tried and true?

Over time, charter advocates have seen an increase in the cap as the main route to allowing tested models and innovative new schools to coexist: More charter school seats could equal more room for risk-taking — except that even the most recent pushes to raise the charter cap have been tied to the idea of authorizing only proven providers. A less frequently discussed mechanism for fostering innovation in the current context has been to allow additional, diverse authorizers to enter the scene.

States looking to the Massachusetts charter experience should consider how to strike a balance between authorizing proven models while also leaving room for new ideas, even if those ideas represent a risk. There are several reasons for this.

First, over time, what is valued in education changes, hopefully for the better, and proven models authorized on the

---

While single authorizers tend to be more risk averse and may therefore authorize high-quality charters, they also have track records of authorizing similar charter schools, which hampers charter diversity and innovation.

premise of producing high test scores might not look as good as they once did. This is not to say that schools authorized because they are proven don't evolve, or even that they only produce high test scores. It is to underscore, however, that authorizers should consistently raise the bar for educational quality over time. One way to do that is to reserve space — in this context, some number of charter school seats — for innovators with new ideas.

Second, when authorizers look only to *replicate* school models, good ideas go elsewhere.[24] Massachusetts has experienced a drain of its educational talent to places with more room for expansion and a less risk-averse approach to charter authorizing. With forethought and purposeful design, a strong charter law and authorizing model can use accountability to ensure excellence and set aside room, even under an undesirable cap, to allow for some number of diverse and innovative school models. To do so is to think not only about the charter school movement today, but also about its future.

LESSON 8:
Charter policy is a legislative matter.

In the lead-up to Question 2, even confident and hopeful charter advocates knew that putting the charter school cap to a public vote was risky. A lawsuit seeking to abolish the cap had recently been dismissed, and charter school politics were already divisive.[25] The context of a campaign "for" or "against" charter schools factionalized the education establishment and the public even further.

The MTA, in its "save our public schools" campaign, was well organized and actively working to protect its members — the reason for the organization's existence. To prevent more charters from being established and the potential loss of union members that would result, the union successfully painted charter schools as harmful to districts. A conversation that could have been about how to better fund all schools or how to make school funding more transparent, turned to "choose us" or "choose them." To a voting public composed mainly of middle class, suburban voters, the choice was clear. No one wants to see their neighborhood school harmed.

It is tempting to wonder what the outcome of Question 2 might have been if more middle class families had access to and used charter schools. If state policies hadn't successfully circumscribed charters as an "escape valve" for students in failing urban districts, would more charters exist in the Commonwealth's wealthier, whiter suburbs? Perhaps, but now that the public has resoundingly voted down a cap lift, it is unlikely that charter school operators will want to open in such communities, even though they are not even close to the cap.

Looking at this most recent experience in Massachusetts, other states should seriously consider which mechanisms to employ to create and grow the charter sector, whether they are at the ballot box, the courthouse, or through their Legislatures. In Massachusetts, charters were conceived in the Legislature and, until 2016, every cap lift was negotiated in the Legislature. While the legislative route hasn't always worked in favor of growing the charter sector or even ensuring its overall health, it has tended to be a reliable and even-handed approach to making charter school seats available where they didn't formerly exist.

The Key to Building a High-Performing Charter Sector

There are important policies to consider when designing a charter law. But to grow a truly robust and high-performing charter sector, policymakers, community members, and educators should be very clear about the purposes of charter schools.

High-performing charter schools and networks across the nation have earned reputations as useful vehicles for turning around failing schools and providing disadvantaged students with options they would not otherwise have. Leveraging charters for certain groups of students or specific reasons is one important component of education reform. But charter schools are important for other reasons as well. First and foremost, they provide families with public school options and, in doing so, empower parents to make one of the most important choices they can for their children: what kind of education they will receive.

Charter schools can also be laboratories of innovation when they are empowered to be. The high-performing charter schools and networks that are now models for school turnaround efforts were once some of the most innovative schools in the country. Without a policy environment that valued innovation, they wouldn't have existed.

Charter school laws and policies that start with an understanding of the purposes of chartering — educational choice, innovation, and quality — and then embrace sound policies that will foster these things produce robust and high-performing charter schools. From these purposes, policymakers can work to ensure that basic aspects of sound charter policy are in place: real autonomy in exchange for real accountability, equal financial footing, no artificial limits on charter school growth, and regulations that favor diversity and competence over replication and compliance are the most important ingredients in any charter school law. Protecting the purposes of chartering by ensuring that these policies are implemented in sound and meaningful ways is critical. This could be the most important lesson learned from the Massachusetts charter school experience.

CHAPTER 8

The Path Ahead:

Charter School Policy and a New Era of Education Reform

E DUCATION REFORM HAS MADE A MEANINGFUL difference for an entire generation of Massachusetts students. More equitable funding, high and measurable standards, and flexible and innovative approaches to operating schools have led to increased literacy, graduation, and college-going rates.

But an enormous amount of work remains: Achievement gaps that have begun to close in some places still exist. Access to high-performing schools still eludes far too many children, especially those who are poor, minority, or speak a primary language other than English. It is wrong to assume that Massachusetts's high standing in national and international rankings means that all students benefit from the academic excellence that exists in some pockets of the Commonwealth. On the contrary, deep inequities persist.

So, what's next? With the Massachusetts Education Reform Act, the Commonwealth managed to shift an educational status quo that accepted low achievement and stunning resource inequities. Now a new status quo has taken hold. It is a better status quo, focused on high standards and a more just approach to funding schools, but it's not good enough. No status quo should ever be good enough.

It's time for a renewed effort to improve public education. That effort should build upon the MERA and provide a new vision of academic excellence — one that includes closing persistent achievement gaps and engaging all students with school. To execute this vision, policymakers must focus on providing both the opportunity for and access to diverse and innovative educational options. The state's charter school sector is a critical lever for implementing a new vision, but it can't be the only one. All the major principles of education reform should be reexamined, reinvented and, where promising, redeployed.

To move forward, we must learn from the past, and the Commonwealth should be wary of allowing the pendulum of reform to swing too far in the wrong direction. Proposals to eliminate MCAS or allow families to opt out of state tests defeat the major purpose of education reform, which was to understand how well public schools serve all students and to ensure accountability for outcomes. Standards and accountability should remain critical components of education reform.

Likewise, the state's investment in schools should remain a top priority. The Legislature should continually reassess its investment in and commitment to all public schools, especially in the poorest communities. Understanding the impacts of Chapter 70 and readjusting it accordingly is important. Fully funding the charter school reimbursement formula is also imperative if the Commonwealth is to remain committed to educational equity. Moreover, taking a close look at how different types of funding (state and local) can be more heavily weighted toward those students (not those schools) with the greatest resource needs could be an integral part of future reforms.

These reforms will continue to make schools more equitable, but equity isn't the only thing to consider in the future. Access to an excellent public education is a prerequisite to equity.

What should children and families have access to? A state-funded education aligned to high academic standards is now a bare minimum expectation. In addition to that, each child and family deserves access to innovative educational options tailored to individual needs

Examining the current charter school movement in Massachusetts is helpful to understanding how the state can create more of the schools that families demand. One obvious way to meet demand for current and future charter school options is to raise or abolish charter schools caps. If only it were that easy.

In the 2018, post-Question 2 environment, any cap-lift seems politically improbable. Defeat at the ballot box is not the only thing charter advocates need to unpack: four charter schools unionized in 2018 and more could follow suit. There is historical precedent for charter school unionization in Massachusetts, but it's not common. When it happens, it is usually indicative of perceptions of instability — often financial — at the school level.

And as school districts steadily increase average teacher pay to make the profession more attractive and retain better teachers, charter school teachers (understandably) look over their shoulders and wonder: "Why shouldn't we get paid more?" The truth is, they should have better pay, but flaws in the state's charter school law negatively impact funding.

The minimal financial support that charter schools receive for facilities makes it nearly impossible to pay teachers what they deserve. Overall budgets are greatly constrained when schools have to pay rent or a mortgage on a facility, forcing school leaders and boards to make difficult decisions about where to put remaining funds. Teachers are a critical resource, and they deserve better pay, but students also require other critical resources and services. Do charter operators prioritize resources for students or adults? Even when the adults serve students, this can be a painful question to answer.

The challenges of the current charter school climate are formidable but not insurmountable. The charter school movement in Massachusetts has never been politically popular, but it has flourished nonetheless. Charter supporters and leaders have doggedly found the political will to expand the movement, one charter school seat at a time. When they've been successful, it hasn't been because of support at the ballot box, but because they've delivered on the promise of better school options.

Of course, eventually raising the charter cap again is neither a magic bullet for better schools nor the only way to leverage the high-performing charters we have now for a better future. Another way to think about the role of charter schools in the next wave of education reform is to take the charter school model of choice, autonomy, and accountability and inject it into the public system at large. This isn't as easy as it sounds, but it is possible. Where the political will does not currently exist to make all schools more autonomous and accountable, it can be cultivated.

To do so, charter school advocates have to be willing to consider improvements to current charter school policy while remaining committed to the original principles of charter schooling. They also have to think beyond a simple sharing of best practices with non-charter schools and be transparent and unabashed about what it takes to achieve excellence for all students in all schools.

The recommendations below, which are intended for policy-makers and education stakeholders in Massachusetts and the nation, address two distinct but complementary approaches to leveraging charter schools as a core part of the next wave of education reform: 1) creating a more robust, diverse, and innovative charter sector; and 2) rethinking how lessons learned from charter schools should influence other public schools.

RECOMMENDATION 1:

Establish equitable facilities funding for charters and a more transparent system of per-pupil funding to benefit all schools

The Commonwealth's charter schools enjoy a higher level of per-pupil funding than other charter public schools nationally, but a lack of access to local property taxes or other state funds forces charter schools to pay for facilities using per-pupil dollars or fundraising. The former takes away from overall school budgets, which negatively impacts students and teachers, and the latter is an unpredictable revenue source.

Allowing charter public schools to access unused public school buildings and/or providing charters with equal and dependable facilities funding by including a more equitable per-pupil facilities allotment is the only way to justly serve families who want a charter school education. Massachusetts charters have earned a reputation for doing more with less, but imagine if they could boost teacher retention with better pay or provide students with the facilities they deserve, such as buildings that include kitchens for hot meals and gyms for in-school and out-of-school activities.

Likewise, if the Chapter 70 funding formula were simplified and transparent, and if the charter school reimbursement formula were fully funded each year, district schools wouldn't feel the "pain" of losing students to charters. Whether charters actually drain funding from district schools matters far less than the perception that they do. The hostility this perception creates prevents needed district-charter collaboration.

Another way to think about more transparently funding all schools is to move to a system that attaches funds to students rather than districts or school buildings. Some communities, like Boston, already weight per-pupil funding to individual student needs. A system that assigns a per-pupil amount to each student according to her needs could then send that amount — derived from state and local sources — to the school of the student's choice. Charter school students would also receive an equitable facilities allotment within their per-pupil allotment. This system, which is already applied in other countries and in some U.S. communities, is simple, transparent, and frames public education as something that belongs to students and families as opposed to education bureaucracies.

RECOMMENDATION 2:

Provide incentives to charter operators to expand to suburban and rural areas

There are several reasons why Massachusetts charter operators have focused on urban centers. First, the greatest demand for charters exists in cities. This is as true of Massachusetts as it is of California or Texas. Additionally, the Commonwealth has passed legislation in recent years that encourages additional growth in urban centers. The 2010 cap-raise in communities already at the cap was necessary, but it also encouraged "proven providers" to replicate the same programs in the same places. This further defined charter schools as a mechanism to serve certain communities (those with schools in need of "turnaround") and certain students (poor and minority).

Some charter schools do exist in suburban areas, and they are most successful when they offer something truly distinct from district schools. Whether immersion in a specific language or access to challenging courses of study in certain disciplines, like math and science, suburban charters fill a need.

The state has done little to encourage charter growth outside of urban centers, and this is one reason why suburbanites, who make up the majority of Massachusetts voters, don't express support for charter public schools. They don't know charter schools because they haven't been exposed to them. Moreover, many are happy with their strong public school options; the mere suggestion that a different kind of school could take anything away from districts — whether true or not — feels threatening.

If suburban voters found value in charter schools, they might be more likely to understand how critical they are to the students and families living in urban centers that have already reached the cap. To expose more middle class families to charter school options, the state should consider working with current and promising charter school operators to design schools that offer distinctive programs in suburban communities.

Charter operators may more easily implement a Montessori

model, for example. Or, they may fill a need by serving "disengaged students." The Phoenix Charter Academies Network has collaborative relationships with districts like Chelsea, Lawrence, and Springfield. The autonomies Phoenix enjoys allow the organization to support certain students in ways a district cannot.

Expanding charter schools in communities not at the cap isn't just about helping the voting public understand what charters have to offer. It is also about encouraging charter operators to expand to communities where there is great need but not necessarily demand for charters.

Alterations to the formula that determines the lowest performing districts in the state were, in part, designed to encourage charter operators to expand outside communities like Boston and into other high-needs communities like Holyoke and Fall River. Unfortunately, changing the formula that determines performance was a political endeavor. To support charter operators expanding to Gateway Cities and even rural communities, the state needs to provide a different kind of incentive.

One of the reasons for establishing a school in a community like Boston is a wealth of human capital. With the greatest concentration of colleges and universities in the nation, Boston's schools can have their pick of bright and talented graduates who could go on to become great teachers. But it can be difficult to convince young graduates to move to smaller communities, especially in rural areas, that cannot offer the amenities of a large urban center. This is why the state could work closely with charter operators to encourage young talent to migrate outside of cities by providing them with pay incentives, housing, or even graduate tuition incentives.

Such programs don't need to be state funded; the Commonwealth could invite collaboration from non-profit partners or provide tax and other incentives for businesses and institutions of higher education to invest in human capital pipelines and resources. Moreover, these relationships and incentives need not apply only to charter operators. They could have important impacts on districts, as well.

RECOMMENDATION 3:

Lift the charter school cap because school choice is a right, not because it is politically popular

Pundits can debate whether it was right to attempt to raise the charter school cap at the ballot box, or whether advocates should have continued to work for a cap-lift through the Legislature or the courts. The debate won't change the outcome of Question 2, but it does highlight a sense of urgency to give the tens of thousands of families on charter school waitlists access to the education of their choice. Some who support charter schools were willing to try anything.

While it is quite possible that the cap the Legislature placed on charter schools in the Education Reform Act led the Commonwealth to develop a conservative and effective approach to authorizing, it is also true that any cap on the number of charter schools is arbitrary and artificial. Charter schools are public schools. Communities would never "cap" the number of public school seats available to residents because it would be illegal and, more importantly, immoral.

In the international context, it is also wrong to deny families the right to the education of their choice. The U.S. is one of the few industrialized countries that confines families to public schools based on where they live. In doing so, it confines families to the public school they can afford. Too often, community resources have a direct relationship to school quality. But charter schools are one very important remedy for this injustice: Commonwealth Charter Schools are districts unto themselves — many draw students from various ZIP codes, and those that currently do not still have that option.

Lifting the charter school cap may be more likely if some of the recommendations described previously are implemented first. A more transparent school funding system and the expansion of charters to communities not at the cap could make a cap-lift less contentious.

But the political conversation about charter schools isn't necessarily the right conversation. Education is a human right, and school choice is an internationally recognized human right. Charter supporters should start talking about abolishing the cap on charter schools, and they should consider abolition of the charter school cap an integral part of the next wave of education reform.

Abolishing the cap on charter schools would not only solve the "demand" problem by allowing more charters. It would also solve what is increasingly a school diversity problem in the Commonwealth. The artificial cap on charter schools comes with a "proven provider" clause in underperforming districts. If the cap did not exist, there would be no need to predict winners and losers. Instead, an authorizer could remain faithful to the core principles of the movement, providing charters with the autonomy they need to be distinctive and successful and hold them accountable, through closure, when they don't produce what they've promised.

In such an environment, proven providers could exist alongside the next charter school innovators. Together, this wider array of charter operators could meet demand and serve a more diverse population.

RECOMMENDATION 4:

Create innovation and diversity in the sector with an independent authorizer

Leading national charter school organizations tout the benefits of multiple charter school authorizers. Having diverse authorizers — such as universities, non-profit organizations, and independent state charter school boards — has led to robust and diverse charter sectors in some states. But Massachusetts has achieved excellence in the charter sector under the oversight of the Board of Elementary and Secondary Education, so why would the state shift course?

It is true that for years the BESE, under the competent guidance of DESE, helped to grow a high-quality charter sector. This is mainly because DESE prioritized providing charters with autonomy and holding them strictly accountable for outcomes. It is also true that neither entity has helped to shepherd the charter sector to grow or become more innovative in the last decade.

In fact, as outlined in the first chapter of this book, it was the former Executive Office of Education (under Governor Bill Weld) that established the conservative approach to authorizing that the Commonwealth employs today. Working under a stringent cap from the beginning, EOE and then-Secretary of Education Michael Sentance realized that "letting a thousand flowers bloom" in the charter sector would not be the right approach for Massachusetts. EOE dug deep to understand indicators of quality. It also valued accountability for outcomes and knew that accountability should be coupled with support.

Though it set the stage for today's charter authorizing, there are also important differences between EOE's approach and the approach DESE takes today. First, although EOE looked for indicators that proposed schools would be successful, it had no incentive to prescribe a charter school model that would favor pre-conceived best practices.

Even without regulations that prioritized proven providers, EOE could have been risk averse. Instead, it balanced authorization of known educational models with new and innovative ones. In the early days of chartering, this resulted in everything from no-excuses schools to schools that embrace project-based learning. In its short tenure, EOE's charter school office approved and authorized what would become some of the nation's highest-performing charter schools.

Second, EOE was an education bureaucracy separate from DESE. Its main function for K–12 education was approving and authorizing charter schools. It could concentrate resources on charters and advocate on behalf of charters. While DESE's charter school office supports charter schools, it is difficult for the larger education bureaucracy to truly advocate for them because it is responsible for all public schools. This larger responsibility means resources are spread broadly and DESE has to maintain an unbiased approach to supporting charter and district schools.

The charter movement in the Commonwealth is at an inflection point. It is not likely that Massachusetts, given its track record of success, would move away from the single-authorizer model. However, it would be a boon to the charter movement to follow the lead of places like Washington, D.C., which also has a very high-performing charter sector. D.C. has one authorizer, an independent Public Charter School Board. The board's sole responsibility is to authorize charter schools.

In Massachusetts, the governor could create and appoint an independent charter school board comprised of individuals with interest and expertise in supporting and growing the Commonwealth's high-quality charter sector. Charter school authorizing, based on the principles DESE has honored — operational autonomy in exchange for strict accountability — would be the board's only function. This board would operate separately from BESE, which would maintain its responsibility for traditional public schools.

Additionally, the charter school office that is currently within DESE (a small but very dedicated group of people) could move from DESE to the independent charter board. The office would continue to do the same strong work it does now — reviewing charter school applications, making recommendations to the board, and overseeing charter school renewal processes — but it would be autonomous. Taking the charter school office out of DESE would ensure more dedicated resources for charters and more independence for the office.

RECOMMENDATION 5:

Keep a steady focus on the right balance of autonomy and accountability

No matter the number of authorizing bodies, the general approach to authorizing should remain the same: Charter schools need autonomy from many of the regulations that apply to districts, and authorizers should prioritize safeguarding that autonomy. Likewise, authorizers must hold charters to a high standard of accountability, closing schools when they fail to meet the terms of their charter.

Traditionally, BESE and DESE have balanced autonomy and accountability in a way that is good for charter operators and good for students and families. But it's not an easy balance to strike. Regulatory bodies tend to err on the side of overregulation, and they sometimes confuse regulation with accountability. Moreover, as educators and policymakers nationwide learn more about the factors and outcomes that predict success later in life, the measures that authorizers use to hold schools accountable are changing.

DESE, in particular, should carefully consider the extent to which routine compliance documents unnecessarily cumbersome charters with paperwork. Over time, applications to open new charter schools and renew charters have grown lengthy and increasingly burdensome. When documents such as these are too long or require operators to provide unnecessary or redundant information, they needlessly distract from the work of operating schools. Likewise, large amounts of paperwork or lengthy application and renewal documents can prevent authorizers from homing in on the critical information they need to understand about charter school performance.

With regard to accountability, BESE, DESE, and any future authorizers should be committed to understanding academic outcomes, financial stability, and the extent to which charter schools are fulfilling their promises and commitments to the communities they serve. This sounds like a simple charge but, in practice, it is becoming increasingly complicated.

As authorizers understand more and more about the K–12 outcomes that predict post secondary and life success, they may hold schools accountable for different and/or additional outcomes. There is mounting evidence that test scores alone (especially scores on criterion-referenced state tests) are skewed predictors of student success. As a result, many authorizers are using multiple measures to understand learning opportunities in each school in addition to student outcomes. Holding schools accountable for access to AP and honors courses and/or outcomes on tests like the SAT or ACT are examples.

Likewise, as authorizers understand more and more about school practices that influence student outcomes, they may desire more day-to-day information about what schools do. State education bureaucracies are increasingly using measures such as rates of out-of-school suspension and chronic absenteeism to hold schools accountable for serving all students. This is appropriate in all contexts, the charter school context included, provided that authorizers are looking to ensure civil rights and equitable access to programs and curricula as opposed to piling on reporting requirements.

Additionally, as charters in Massachusetts diversify, they should also serve more diverse student populations, which may impact how authorizers think about accountability. If a charter chooses, for example, to serve students who have dropped out of school or are at risk of dropout, should that school be accountable if it has high rates of chronic absenteeism? Or, if a school chooses to serve students who are also parents, should that school be accountable for getting all students to graduation within four or five years?

By design, some innovative schools — charter or otherwise — will exist to serve students who have extreme difficulty excelling on certain measures. In these cases, authorizers should work closely with the schools to support them in defining appropriate accountability measures that will hold charter operators to high but realistic expectations.

As the Massachusetts charter sector matures and expands, it will change. To meet shifting needs, the type and number of things for which charters are held accountable may also change. Accountability should be tailored to some extent, but the core principle of accountability that has guided the Commonwealth's charter school movement should remain the same. Authorizers should: 1) focus on maintaining high standards for schools; 2) seek to understand school outputs as opposed to inputs; and 3) close charter schools when they fail to meet the performance criteria outlined in their charters.

RECOMMENDATION 6:

Beyond best practice: apply lessons from charter schools to districts

The MERA envisioned that charter schools would be laboratories for change that could provide valuable lessons for all public schools. Many of the "innovations" that are increasingly common in district schools — extended school days, additional "time on learning," and data-driven instruction — were born in charter schools. Yet critics charge that charters have done little to share best practices.

In Massachusetts there is a political divide between charters and districts, and that divide contributes to the perception that charters and districts are unhealthy (rather than healthy) competitors. In painting charters as a financial drain on traditional schools, districts have done little to endear themselves to charter operators. Conversely, some charter operators have almost single-mindedly focused on the students in front of them, failing to take the time to consider how their successful practices could be implemented elsewhere.

Additionally, districts understand that much of what charters do hinges upon the autonomies that they have. When charters have the freedom to hire a particular teaching staff or extend the school day and year (many districts struggle to do this), it is easier for them to bake additional learning time into the day, dedicate resources to personalizing student learning, and keep a highly qualified teaching staff.

But ease of implementation shouldn't stand in the way. In fact, if charters did a better job explaining *why* their autonomy makes a difference for students, more districts might advocate for those autonomies, even when they face powerful teachers' unions and prescriptive collective bargaining agreements. Charters should also do a better job of inviting district schools in — helping a more diverse array of school and teacher leaders understand how they leverage their autonomies.

Of course, collaboration requires that all parties have something to give. Massachusetts's charters are incredibly successful, but in the past decade they have begun to serve more diverse student populations. Many districts — especially large, urban districts — have deep experience serving students with a variety of special needs. Charters would do well to look to successful districts as they think through the programs, services, and supports they provide.

There are also other reasons for charters to look to district schools. Most charters are located in urban centers but aim to have their students access the same post secondary opportunities that students in wealthy suburbs commonly have. Understanding how successful suburban schools prepare students to succeed (academically and otherwise) in competitive colleges could help charter students.

Well-intentioned groups have for some time tried to facilitate the sharing of "best practices" between charters and districts, and some have succeeded. Generally speaking, however, there is more work to be done. Charters and districts must get beyond the idea that school visits and collegiality are enough. Instead, they should consider working together to develop strong teacher training programs and human capital pipelines. Cross-sector professional development for school and teacher leaders is effective but not common. If it happened more often it could impact the political divide that clouds charter/district collaboration.

RECOMMENDATION 7:

Apply charter school accountability practices to all public schools

Another way of thinking about the potential impact of charter schools on districts is to consider what might happen if all schools were as accountable for student outcomes as charter schools are. Massachusetts charters have to continually renew their good standing with the state. The five-year authorization cycle means charter operators are laser focused on outcomes; if they don't achieve the outcomes they promise, their school could cease to exist.

While all public schools in Massachusetts are accountable for student outcomes under the MERA, the stakes for districts and charters are different. The Commonwealth collects data on student test scores, dropout rates, and even out-of-school suspension rates. District schools can perform poorly on one or more of these measures and receive a mediocre or failing grade from the state. But even if that failing grade persists for a long period of time, district schools rarely face closure.

Only after a school or district has dramatically under-served students over a long period does the state step in and provide resources that can help turn around the school. And turnaround efforts don't always result in the change students need. The Commonwealth has seen everything from successful turnarounds of entire districts to turnaround schools that perpetually struggle to help students achieve basic outcomes. And it's important to note that in the most successful district turnaround to date — Lawrence — the district looked carefully at the charter school sector to understand how it might improve its schools.

If they were subject to charter-like accountability, districts would operate under a different set of incentives that might foster success. If districts had to renew their standing with the state every five years, proving via data and school inspections that they were serving students well, underperformance might be flagged before an entire generation of students falls through the cracks. If school and district leaders constantly had to think holistically about the extent to which they were fulfilling a stated mission while also meeting promises they made about student achievement, access to learning opportunities, and family engagement, they might react sooner to indicators of poor performance.

The caveat to this, critics will argue, is that district schools can't just close when they fail to perform; where will the students go? This line of thinking demonstrates just how entrenched most of us are in the status quo. If schools persistently fail students, they should be closed so that different and perhaps better schools can take their place. If a given group of adults is not able to adequately serve the students in front of them, another group of adults should be trusted to provide those students with an education. Closing schools and opening better ones in their place does not require new facilities or the migration of students from one place to another (though it could if parents so desire). It requires a new way of thinking about academic success, a new way of doing things and, in most cases, a new group of highly trained, highly accountable adults who can help students achieve their potential.

This is how it works in the charter sector. This is how it works in other countries that embrace accountability for outcomes, school choice, and the idea that every student deserves not just an adequate education but an excellent one. This could work in Massachusetts, but it requires a fundamentally different mindset, one that recognizes that education is about students, not schools and systems.

CONCLUSION:
The path ahead

Massachusetts is a leader in education reform. It has enshrined in law its commitment to social justice through educational opportunity. In the charter school sector, it has given decision-making power to the educational stakeholders — teachers, school leaders, and parents — who understand what is best for children. But the work is not nearly done. It is time for a new wave of education reform. Understanding the state of education reform today is a critical step to moving forward.

Charter schools are one of the great education reform success stories. Charter schools in Massachusetts, and particularly in Boston, work better than any other group of public schools in the nation. With the right autonomy and accountability for outcomes, the Commonwealth's charter schools have provided innovative, high-quality options for the students who need them most. Charters have also provided a model for all public schools in the state. Some communities have completely reversed declines in their public schools by applying the basic principles of charter schooling — enhanced autonomy and enhanced accountability — to districts.

The Commonwealth's charter school movement should expand, and over time it will. But it is up to the people and the Legislature to ensure that the integrity and spirit of the movement remain intact. Charter schools are one important lever for turning around failing schools and districts. They can act as an "escape valve" for families who don't have other strong public school options. But they can and must be much more than that. Charter schools are about innovation and choice. Over the past 20 years they have produced countless school leaders, teachers, students, and families with an alternative way of thinking about school "systems."

The next 20 years of the charter school movement should put the concept of education reform to the test. Will charter schools remain a "boutique" option for a fortunate subset of students and remain confined mainly to urban centers? Or will we find the political will to expand not only charter schools but also the policies that make them strong? Education reform will have succeeded, in part, if it has a much broader impact on the status quo; forcing schools and districts to push decision-making power down from bureaucracies to school leaders, teachers, families and students.

And there is also a bigger, more fundamental question at play. We should ask "How do we create more charter schools?" and "How do we create more charter-like policies?" But we should also ask, again and again until we find a satisfactory answer, "How do we understand public education?" Is it something provided by communities, based on a ZIP code and the relative wealth that comes with it? Or is education and the choice to decide the kind of education a student will receive a fundamental right, something that all parents deserve?

When the Commonwealth embraces the stance that school choice and access to excellent and innovative educational options is something every family deserves, regardless of income, education reform will have begun to reach its true potential.

Endnotes

CHAPTER 1
A Brief History of Charter Schooling in Massachusetts

1. Peterson, Paul and West, Martin (2007), "The Adequacy Lawsuit: A Critical Appraisal," in *School Money Trials*, The Brookings Institution Press, p. 7.

2. Jami McDuffy & others vs. Secretary of the Executive Office of Education & others; 415 Mass. 545.

3. The seven capabilities outlined by the SJC are: 1) sufficient oral and written communication skills; 2) sufficient knowledge of economic, social, and political systems; 3) sufficient understanding of governmental process; 4) sufficient self-knowledge of his or her mental and physical wellness; 5) sufficient grounding in the arts; 6) sufficient training or presentation for advanced studies; and, 7) sufficient level of academic or vocational skills.

4. Flint, Anthony, "Democrats Unveil Plan for School Reform: Could Cost $1B, Kill Decrease in State Income Tax," *The Boston Globe*, November 26, 1991.

5. "Demystifying the Chapter 70 Formula: How the Massachusetts Education Funding System Works," (2010), massbudget.org, http://www.massbudget.org/report_window.php?loc=Facts_10_22_10.html.

6. Budde, Ray (1996) "The Evolution of the Charter Concept," *Phi Delta Kappan* 78(1), p.1.

7. Budde, Ray (1996) "The Evolution of the Charter Concept" *Phi Delta Kappan* 78(1), p.1.

8. Peterson, Paul (2010), "No, Al Shanker did not invent the charter school," *Education Next*, http://educationnext.org/no-al-shanker-did-not-invent-the-charter-school/.

9. Interview with Senator Thomas Birmingham, April 25, 2017.

10. Interview with Steven F. Wilson, Oct. 9, 2009.

11. Stein Charles, "Bill Edgerly's New Crusade," *The Boston Globe*, May 16, 1993.

12. Interview with Steven F. Wilson, Oct. 9, 2009.

13. Gustafson, Joey (2013), "Charter authorizers face challenges: Quality control takes money and staff," *Education Next* 13(3).

14. "National Charter School Laws Ranking and Scorecard" (2017), Center for Education Reform, https://www.edreform.com/issues/choice-charter-schools/laws-legislation/.

15. Unlike district schools, charter schools cannot draw from local property taxes in the communities where they are located. Per-pupil charter school tuition rates are determined by the Department of Elementary and Secondary Education and designed to reflect the per-pupil tuition rates of the sending district (districts that charter school students would otherwise attend). In determining tuition rates, the state also accounts for the needs of charter school students, just as it accounts for the needs of district school students. Special education and socio-economic status, for example, can impact the tuition rate associated with each student/group of students.

16. Batdorf et. al (2014) "Charter School Funding: Inequity Expands," School Choice Demonstration Project, University of Arkansas, http://www.uaedreform.org/wp-content/uploads/charter-funding-inequity-expands.pdf; Grover, Lisa (2016) "Facilities funding for charter public schools," National Alliance for Charter Public Schools, http://www.publiccharters.org/publications/facilities-funding-for-charter-schools-2016/.

17. Ardon, Ken & Candal, Cara (2016) "Assessing Charter School Funding in 2016," Pioneer Institute white paper no. 148.

18. Gillespie, Nick, Keisling, Jason, & Snell, Lisa, "5 Facts About Charter Schools," *Reason.com*, January 28, 2015.

19. Hart, Jordana, "Funding Charter Schools Proves Bitter Topic," *The Boston Globe*, February 27, 1995.

20. Massachusetts Department of Elementary and Secondary Education, "Charter School Fact Sheet."

21. Interview with Michael Sentance, September 11, 2009.

22. Massachusetts Department of Elementary and Secondary Education, "Charter School Fact Sheet."

23. Candal (2009), "Putting Children First."

24. Kirby, Ed. "Breaking Regulatory Barriers to Reform" in Hess, Frederick, M. (Ed.) Educational Entrepreneurship: Possibilities for School Reform (2008), Harvard Education Press, Cambridge, MA, pp. 207–224.

25. Candal (2009), "Putting Children First."

26. "Schools at the Top of the Hill," *The Economist*, February 22, 1997.

27. Zernike, Kate, "Panel backs adding of charter schools; Bill allows changes at existing schools,"*The Boston Globe*, June 25, 1997.

28. Interview with Karin Wall, April 14, 2017.

29. Candal (2009) "Putting Children First."

30. In 2008, then-Governor Deval Patrick reestablished and reformed the Executive Office of Education and expanded the responsibilities of the then-Board of Education. Under this reorganization, the BOE became the Board of Elementary and Secondary Education (BESE). BESE has been the Commonwealth's charter school authorizer since that time. See: "Reville named state secretary of education," UMASS Amherst, "News and Media Relations," Press Release, March 12, 2008.

31. Massachusetts Department of Elementary and Secondary Education, "Questions and Answers about Charter Schools in Massachusetts," http://www.doe.mass.edu/charter/about.html.

32. Massachusetts Education Reform Act, Chapter 71, Section 89.

33. Massachusetts Department of Elementary and Secondary Education, "Charter School Fact Sheet and Closure History," http://www.doe.mass.edu/charter/about.html.

34. The 2001 reauthorization of the Elementary and Secondary Education Act (ESEA), *No Child Left Behind,* required all states to develop state standards in core subject areas and state tests to ensure that standards were being taught and mastered.

35. MGL, Chapter 12, Section 7(3).

36. Lannan, Katie "Governor Baker Featured In a New Ad as Charter Backers Look to Mobilize Voters," State House News Service, October 25, 2016, http://www.masslive.com/politics/index.ssf/2016/10/gov_charlie_baker_featured_in.html.

37. "Charter question splits suburbs, even suburbs with no charter schools," WBUR, Edify, http://www.wbur.org/edify/2016/11/03/charter-question-two-suburbs.

38. Interview with Karin Wall.

CHAPTER 2

Supply and Demand: Profiles of Charter Schools and Their Students

1. Massachusetts Department of Elementary and Secondary Education, "Charter school fact sheet, directory, and application history."

2. Reville, Paul & Coggins, Celine (Eds.)(2007) *A Decade of Urban School Reform: Progress and Persistence in the Boston Public Schools,* Harvard Education Press, Cambridge.

3. Candal, Cara (Ed.)(2009) *Partnering for Progress: Boston University, The Chelsea Public Schools, and Urban Education Reform,* Information Age Press, Charlotte.

4. Whitmeyer, Richard (2016) *The Founders: Inside the Revolution to Invent (and Reinvent) America's Best Charter Schools,* the74million.org.

5. Toppo, Greg (2015) "Catholic schools seek innovative ways to reduce slide," USA Today, https://www.usatoday.com/story/news/nation/2015/09/16/catholic-schools-decline-pope-francis-visit-us/72327016/.

6. Whitman, David (2008) *Sweating the Small Stuff: Inner City Schools and the New Paternalism,* The Thomas B. Fordham Institute.

7. Thernstrom & Thernstrom (2003) *No Excuses: Closing the Racial Gap in Learning,* Simon and Schuster, New York.

8. Massachusetts Regulations on Charter Schools: 603 CMR 1.00, section 1.05.

9. See Ardon & Candal (2016) "Students with Special Educational Needs in Massachusetts Charter Schools, Demographic and Achievement Trends," Pioneer Institute white paper no. 155.

10. ibid.

11. ibid.

12. Fergus, Edward (2010) "Common causes of the over identification of racial/ethnic minorities in special education: understanding and addressing disproportionality," The Special Edge, (23), http://www. calstat.org/publications/article_detail.php?a_id=128&nl_id=19.

13. "Truth in labeling: disproportionality in special education," National Education Association," 2007, http://www.nea.org/assets/ docs/HE/EW-TruthInLabeling.pdf.

14. Excel Academies, "Excel Academy History," http://www.excel-academy.org/history/; Match Charter Schools, "About Us," http:// www.matchschool.org/about/about-us/; "Our History," http:// phoenixcharteracademy.org/who-we-are/our-history/.

15. Massachusetts Department of Elementary and Secondary Education, School and District Profiles, 2014–15.

16. Ardon & Candal (2016) "English language learners in Massachusetts Charter Schools, Demographic and Achievement Trends," Pioneer Institute white paper no. 156.

17. ibid.

18. Setren, Elizabeth (2015) Special Education and English Language Learner Students in Boston Charter Schools: Impact and Classification, pp. 15–16.

19. ibid.

20. Setren, Elizabeth (2015) Special Education and English Language Learner Students in Boston Charter Schools: Impact and Classification, A-13.

21. "Charter School Success? Or Selective Out-Migration of Low-Achievers? Effects of Enrollment Management on Student Achievement (2009) Center for Education Policy and Practice, Massachusetts Teachers Association, p. 2.

22. ibid.

23. MA DESE "About the Data," "Profiles Help," http://profiles.doe.mass. edu/help/data.aspx?section=students.

24. Massachusetts Department of Elementary and Secondary Education (2016), "Charter school enrollment data annual report," p. 12, http://www.doe.mass.edu/research/reports/2016/02Charter-Report.pdf.

25. See, for example: "Informing the debate: comparing Boston's charter, pilot, and traditional schools," (January, 2009), American Institutes for Research, Washington, D.C.; "Charter school performance in Massachusetts," (2013), Center for Research on Educational Outcomes (CREDO), Stanford University; Setren, Elizabeth (2015) Special Education and English Language Learner Students in Boston Charter Schools: Impact and Classification.

26. Setren, Elizabeth (2015) Special Education and English Language Learner Students in Boston Charter Schools: Impact and Classification.

CHAPTER 3
Outcomes: Measuring the Success of Massachusetts Charter Schools

1. Massachusetts Education Reform Act, Chapter 71, Section 89.

2. Whitmeyer, Richard (2016) *The Founders: Inside the Revolution to Invent (and Reinvent) America's Best Charter Schools,* the74million.org.

3. Thernstrom & Thernstrom (2003) *No Excuses: Closing the Racial Gap in Learning,* Simon and Schuster, New York.

4. Massachusetts Department of Education, Report of the Massachusetts Charter School Initiative, 1996, p. 37.

5. Massachusetts Department of Education, Report of the Massachusetts Charter School Initiative, 2001, p. 66.

6. Hernandez, Raymond, "Charter schools gaining support," *The New York Times,* February 28, 1998.

7. Pilot schools, created in 2000, are Boston district schools that have been granted some but not all of the same autonomies as charter schools. They can, for example, extend the school day, but do not have the same autonomies around hiring and firing staff, etc.

8. Abdulkadiroglu et. al (2009) "Informing the debate: Comparing Boston's charter, pilot, and traditional schools," The Boston Foundation, p. 9.

9. Center for Research on Educational Outcomes (CREDO) (2013) "National Charter School Study" Stanford University.

10. National Academy of Education, *High school dropout, graduation, and completion rates* (2011) National Academies Press, p. 43.

11. Massachusetts Department of Education, Data Overview of the Dropouts in Massachusetts 2015–16, available at http://www.doe.mass.edu/infoservices/reports/dropout/2015-2016.

12. Massachusetts Department of Education, graduation rates available at http://profiles.doe.mass.edu/state_report/gradrates.aspx.

13. Roderick, Melissa (1994), "Grade retention and school dropout: Investigating the association," *American Educational Research Journal,* 31(4), pp. 721–759.

14. City on a Hill Charter Public Schools 2014–15 Annual Report, http://www.cityonahill.org/wp-content/uploads/2015/08/City-on-a-Hill-2014-15-Annual-Report-Final.pdf, accessed October 10, 2016.

15. Angrist et. al (2016) "Stand and Deliver: Effects of Boston's Charter High Schools on College Preparation, Entry, and Choice," *Journal of Labor Economics* 34(2).

16. ibid.

17. "Massachusetts Advanced Placement gains lead the nation," Massachusetts Department of Elementary and Secondary Education press release, February 26, 2016. Accessed October 4, 2016.

18. Tappo, Greg "Charter schools' thorny problem: Few students go on to earn college degrees," *USA Today*, March 14, 2017, https://www.usatoday.com/story/news/2017/03/14/charter-schools-college-degrees/99125468/.

19. Author's calculations using data from http://profiles.doe.mass.edu/state_report/ap_part.aspx National Center for Education Statistics, "Fast Facts," "Elementary and Secondary Education Enrollment."

20. Author's calculations using data from http://profiles.doe.mass.edu/state_report/ap_part.aspx.

21. Boston Collegiate Charter School Website, "College Readiness Programming," http://bostoncollegiate.org/100/college-readiness.html.

22. Levenson, Michael "College graduation rates for Boston students are up, but that's not the whole picture," *The Boston Globe*, June 14, 2016.

23. ibid.

24. Weissman, Jordan (2012) "Why do so many Americans drop out of college? How America's higher education system became one big dropout factory," *The Atlantic*, https://www.theatlantic.com/business/archive/2012/03/why-do-so-many-americans-drop-out-of-college/255226/.

25. Most schools pay to access data from the National Student Clearinghouse — a non-government institution that tracks, among other things, college enrollment and graduation. To account for inaccuracies in this database, however, many schools and networks supplement Clearinghouse data with their own tracking and records.

26. Whitmire, Richard (2017), "Data show charter school students graduating from college at three to five times national average," *The 74 Million*, https://www.the74million.org/article/exclusive-data-shows-charter-school-students-graduating-college-at-three-to-five-times-national-average/.

27. The "Save Our Public Schools" campaign, funded almost entirely by the Massachusetts Teachers Association, is an example of the narrative that has been produced in the argument against charter schools. During the contentious debate over Question 2, the ballot measure to raise the charter school cap, the opposition advanced the notion that charters drain money from public schools (though charter schools are public) and claimed that the initiative to raise the cap was promulgated by wealthy investors from outside of the state looking to make a profit on charter school expansion. The veracity of such claims aside, the opposition convinced the voting public, which overwhelmingly voted against raising the charter school cap.

28. Massachusetts Department of Elementary and Secondary Education, "Questions and answers about charter schools in Massachusetts," http://www.doe.mass.edu/charter/about.html.

29. Horace Mann charters do not enjoy all of the same autonomies as their Commonwealth counterparts.

CHAPTER 4

Leveraging Autonomy: How High-Performing Charter Schools Get Results

1. In states where unions have direct authorizing authority, charters are rarely granted the basic autonomies that they need to differentiate themselves. In other states, charters may be granted basic autonomies under law but districts retain the right to either grant or strip charters of the autonomies that they may have. In still other scenarios with district authorizers, the law may grant charters autonomy that districts are not supposed to take away. In practice, however, when districts curtail charter autonomy, charter schools have no recourse to question district decisions—this happens in states where districts are sole authorizers and the law builds in no oversight for authorizers. See: Allen, Jeanne, Consoletti, Allison, Kerwin, Kara (2012) "The essential guide for charter school lawmaking: Model legislation for states," Center for Education

Reform, https://www.edreform.com/wp-content/uploads/2012/10/CER-ModelCharterLegislation.pdf.

2. Interview with Todd Sumner, Francis W. Parker Charter Essential School, January 9, 2015, in Candal, Cara (2015) "Great teachers are not born, they are made," Pioneer Institute white paper no. 130; Francis W. Parker Charter Essential School, "Learn about our program," "Program summary," https://www.theparkerschool.org/about/learn-more-about-parker/.

3. Mathews, Jay (2004) "Portfolio assessment: Can it be used to hold students accountable?" *Education Next* 4(3).

4. Academy of the Pacific Rim Charter Public School, "About APR," "Why APR?" http://www.pacrim.org/apps/pages/index.jsp?uREC_ID=89050&type=d&termREC_ID=&pREC_ID=168566.

5. Codman Academy Charter Public School, "History," http://www.codmanacademy.org/apps/pages/index.jsp?uREC_ID=238433&type=d.

6. Interview with Thabiti Brown, Head of School, Codman Academy, November 5, 2012.

7. Codman Academy, "Success," "Awards," http://www.codmanacademy.org/apps/pages/index.jsp?uREC_ID=238594&type=d.

8. Candal, Cara (2015) "Massachusetts charter public schools: Best practices serving English language learners," Pioneer Institute white paper no. 140.

9. This profile of Match Charter Public School derives from: Candal, Cara (2014) "Match-ing students to excellent tutors: How one Massachusetts charter school bridges achievement gaps," Pioneer Institute white paper no. 110.

10. Match now operates three schools in Boston (Match Community Day, Match Middle School, and Match High School). Combined, those schools serve students in grades pre-K to 12. All Match schools offer high dosage tutoring for every student.

11. Kraft, Matthew A. (2013), "How to make additional time matter: integrating individualized tutorials into an extended day." Unpublished paper, Harvard Graduate School of Education.

12. Match Education, "Prior projects," "District partnerships," http://www.matcheducation.org/export/prior-projects/district-partnerships/.

13. Candal, Cara (2016) "Massachusetts charter public schools: best practices in curricular innovation," Pioneer Institute white paper no. 141.

14. Teachers Matter, (2015) Rand Policy Brief, http://www.rand.org/content/dam/rand/pubs/corporate_pubs/2012/RAND_CP69 3z1-2012-09.pdf.

15. Chetty, Friedman, and Rockoff (2011) "The long-term impacts of teachers: teacher value-added and student outcomes in adulthood," NBER Working Paper, 17699. Quotes cited here downloaded from http://www.nber.org/papers/w17699, January 16, 2015.

16. National Council on Teacher Quality (NCTQ) (2014) "New report from the National Council on Teacher Quality gives Massachusetts improved grades for policies that support effective teaching," press release downloaded from http://www.nctq.org/dmsView/2013_State_Teacher_Policy_Yearbook_Massachusetts_Press_Release, accessed January 24, 2015.

17. Education Trust (2013), "Dispelling the Myth: Edward Brooke Charter School, Roslindale," https://edtrust.org/resource/dtm-edward-brooke-charter-roslindale/.

18. Osborne, David and Langhorne, Emily "Let schools judge teachers: Effective teacher evaluation happens without central mandates," U.S. News & World Report, August 29, 2017.

19. Vaznis, James, "Most Boston charter schools reject performance-based pay for teachers." The Boston Globe, September 23, 2017.

20. Candal, Cara (2015) "Great teachers are not born, they are made," Pioneer Institute white paper no. 130.

21. Interview with Joseph McCleary, Executive Director, Advanced Math and Science Academy, September 15, 2015.

22. Massachusetts Department of Education, "Charter school fact sheet, directory, and application history," http://www.doe.mass.edu/charter/about.html.

23. Candal, Cara (2016) "Massachusetts charter public schools: Best practices in character education," Pioneer Institute white paper no. 149.

24. Supovitz, J.A. & Christman, J.B. (2005). "Small learning communities that actually learn: Lessons for school leaders," *Phi Delta Kappan*, 86(9), 649–651; Howley, C., Strange, M., & Bickel, R. (2000). "Research about school size and school performance in impoverished communities." (Report No. EDO-RC-00-01).

25. Center for Research on Educational Outcomes (CREDO) (2015) "Urban charter school study report on 41 regions," https://urbancharters.stanford.edu/download/Urban%20Charter%20School%20Study%20Report%20on%2041%20Regions.pdf.

26. Candal, Cara (2016) "Massachusetts charter public schools: Best practices in character education," Pioneer Institute white paper no. 149.

27. Candal, Cara (2014) "Match-ing students to excellent tutors: How one Massachusetts charter school bridges achievement gaps," Pioneer Institute white paper no. 110.

CHAPTER 5

Follow the Money: Charter School Funding and Its Impacts

1. Massachusetts General Law, Part I, Title XII, Chapter 70, "School funds and state aid for public schools."

2. For an overview and history of state charter school laws: Center for Education Reform, "National Charter School Law Ranking and Scorecard," editions 1 – 17, https://www.edreform.com/2017/06/national-charter-school-law-ranking-scorecard/.

3. MGL, Chapter 70.

4. See Massachusetts General Law, Chapter 71; also, Ardon, Ken and Candal, Cara (2016), "Charter School Funding in 2016," Pioneer Institute white paper no. 148.

5. Dynarski et al. (2010) "Charter schools: a report on rethinking the federal role in education," Brookings Institution, https://www.brookings.edu/research/charter-schools-a-report-on-re-thinking-the-federal-role-in-education/; see also: Batdorf et al. (2014) "Charter school funding: Inequity expands," School Choice Demonstration Project, University of Arkansas, http://www.uaedreform.org/wp-content/uploads/charter-funding-in-equity-expands.pdf; Grover, Lisa (2016) "Facilities funding for charter public schools," National Alliance for Charter Public Schools, http://www.publiccharters.org/publications/facilities-funding-for-charter-schools-2016/.

6. Candal, "Putting Children First."

7. ibid.

8. Adapted from Massachusetts Department of Elementary and Secondary Education, "Understanding district aid for Common-wealth charter school tuition," http://www.doe.mass.edu/charter/finance/tuition/reimbursements.html.

9. Massachusetts Department of Elementary and Secondary Education, "Understanding district aid forCommonwealth charter school tuition," accessed June, 2018, http://www.doe.mass.edu/charter/finance/tuition/reimbursements.html.

10. See Camera, Lauren, "Massachusetts plays host to renewed charter school debate," *U.S. News & World Report*, September 27, 2016.

11. Estimate based on data provided in: Massachusetts Department and Elementary and Secondary Education, "FTE tuition and reimbursement profile, FY 96 to present.

12. All data provided in this report derive from publicly available records from the Massachusetts Department of Elementary and Secondary Education. Some analysis and estimates included in Ardon & Candal, 2016, are also presented here.

CHAPTER 6
A Losing Proposition: The Best Charter Schools in the Nation v. the Status Quo

1. McNeill, Claire, "Mass senate rejects bill to raise charter school limit," *The Boston Globe*, July 16, 2014, http://www.bostonglobe. com/metro/2014/07/16/senate-rejects-bill-raise-charter-school-limit/OVCWaku4zU7hDFNYy1IiTM/story.html?event=event12.

2. Schoenberg, Shira, "Massachusetts senate passes controversial charter school bill," Masslive, April 7, 2016, http://www.masslive.com/politics/index.ssf/2016/04/massachusetts_senate_passes_co.html.

3. "Charlie Baker and Karen Polito support raising cap on charter schools" July 14, 2014, https://patch.com/massachusetts/westford/charlie-baker-and-karyn-polito-support-raising-cap-on-charter-schools.

4. Ballotpedia, "Massachusetts authorization of additional charter schools," https://ballotpedia.org/Massachusetts_Authorization_of_Additional_Charter_Schools_and_Charter_School_Expansion,_Question_2_(2016). https://ballotpedia.org/Massachusetts_Authorization_of_Additional_Charter_Schools_and_Charter_School_Expansion,_Question_2_(2016).

5. O'Sullivan, Jim, "Charter school advocates launch $18 million effort," *The Boston Globe*, January 11, 2016.

6. Interview with Keri Rodrigues, former Massachusetts State Director, Families for Excellent Schools.

7. McCambridge, Ruth "Charter school advocates struggle to overcome damage of dark money," Non-Profit Quarterly, February 12, 2018, https://nonprofitquarterly.org/2018/02/12/charter-school-advocates-struggle-overcome-damage-dark-money/.

8. Jonas, Michael, "Suburbs and the charter school question," *Commonwealth Magazine*, May 7, 2016, https://commonwealthmagazine.org/education/suburbs-and-the-charter-school-question/.

9. Boston Teachers Union, "Charter schools: the promise, the hype, and the reality," https://btu.org/hot-issues/charter-schools/.

10. Danilova, Maria & Swanson, Emily, "AP/NORC poll: most Americans feel fine about school choice," US News & World Report, May 12, 2017.

11. Massachusetts Department of Elementary and Secondary Education, "Charter school fact sheet, directory, and application history," http://www.doe.mass.edu/charter/about.html.

12. Interview with Tim Nicolette, Executive Director, Massachusetts Charter Public Schools Association, November 27, 2017.

13. "Citizens for Public Schools," "More than 100 MA school committees say "no" on question 2, https://www.citizensforpublicschools.org/more-than-100-ma-school-committees-say-no-on-question-2/.

14. Correspondence with Dom Slowey, June 1, 2018.

15. Interview with Dawn Tillman, May 10, 2017.

16. McNerny, Kathleen & Chakrabarty, Megna "Unmasking the dark money behind charter school ballot question," September 15, 2016, http://www.wbur.org/radioboston/2017/09/15/dark-money.

17. Shapiro, Eliza, "Families for Excellent Schools to close following CEO's firing," politico.com, February 5, 2018, https://www.politico.com/states/new-york/albany/story/2018/02/05/families-for-excellent-schools-planning-to-close-following-ceos-firing-235707.

18. Larkin, Max, "Where the money comes from in the fight over charter schools," October 27, 2016, http://www.wbur.org/edify/2016/10/27/where-the-money-comes-from-in-the-fight-over-charter-schools.

19. Interview with Keri Rodrigues.

20. Miller, Yawu, "Thousands rally in Boston Common for Boston's public schools," The Bay State Banner, May 24, 2017, http://baystatebanner.com/news/2017/may/24/thousands-rally-boston-common-bostons-public-schoo/.

21. Disare, Monica, "'No Excuses', No More? Charter schools rethink discipline after focus on tough consequences," Chalkbeat, March 17, 2016.

22. Thernstrom & Thernstrom (2003) *No Excuses: Closing the Racial Gap in Learning*, Simon and Schuster, New York.

23. Herrnstein, Richard, J. & Murray, Charles (1994), *The Bell Curve: Intelligence and Class Structure in American Life*, University of Toronto.

24. Whitman, David (2008) *Sweating the Small Stuff: Inner City Schools and the New Paternalism*, The Thomas B. Fordham Institute.

25. McShane & Hatfield (2015), "Measuring Diversity in Charter School Offerings," American Enterprise Institute, p. 9. In this study the authors searched school websites and categorized each school's approach based on the available description. Of the 25 Boston charter schools surveyed, 17 were identified as "general," three as "progressive," and two as "no excuses." The authors reserved the "general" categorization for schools that do not promote a specific specialization, such as STEM. Arguably, schools could adopt one or many elements of a no-excuses approach and fall into the "general" category in this study if they did not mention certain practices associated with no-excuses schools on their websites.

26. Angrist (2013).

27. Fryer, Roland, G. Injecting Charter School Best Practices into Traditional Public Schools: Evidence From Field Experiments. *Quarterly Journal of Economics* (2014). 2014; 129 (3): 1355–1407.

28. Candal, Cara, (2014) "Innovation Interrupted: How the Achievement Gap Act of 2010 has redefined charter public schooling in Massachusetts," Pioneer Institute white paper no. 148.

29. Massachusetts General Law (MGL) Acts of 2010, Chapter 12.

30. Massachusetts Department of Elementary and Secondary Education, Charter School Fact Sheet, http://www.doe.mass.edu/charter/about.html.

31. See: Candal, "Putting Children First."

32. Vaznis, James "Panel's vote reaffirms charter school formula," *The Boston Globe*, June 24, 2014.

33. ibid.

34. Interview with Harneen Chernow, Massachusetts Board of Elementary and Secondary Education, October 5, 2014.

35. Memo to the Board of Elementary and Secondary Education from Mitchell D. Chester, Commissioner of Education, Massachusetts, June 20, 2014.

36. Wood, Peter, "The wake-me-up-when-class-is-over governor: Deval Patrick chooses teachers' union votes over effective schools," National Review, January 24, 2008.

37. Interview with Bruce Bean, data manager, The Community Group, October 14, 2014.

38. Massachusetts Department of Elementary and Secondary Education, "Districts subject to increases in the charter school cap, 2018," http://www.doe.mass.edu/charter/about.html.

39. See: Candal, Cara (2014) "Matching students to excellent tutors: How a Massachusetts charter school bridges achievement gaps," Pioneer Institute white paper no. 110.

40. Interview with Marc Kenen, Former Executive Director, Massachusetts Charter Public School Association, Sept. 29, 2014.

41. Interview with Ed Kirby, October 5, 2014.

42. Interview with James Peyser, April 9, 2013.

CHAPTER 7

Lessons Learned: Charter School Policy and the Massachusetts Experience

1. Massachusetts Department of Elementary and Secondary Education (2016) "Charter school fact sheet."

2. Ibid (this number represents unique students on waitlists).

3. Lovenheim, Michael & Willem, Alexander (2016) "How teacher collective bargaining affects students' employment and earnings later in life," Education Next, Winter 16(1) http://educationnext.org/bad-bargain-teacher-collective-bargaining-employment-earnings/.

4. See, for example, Wong, Audrye (2014) "State charter law and charter school outcomes," *Michigan Journal of Public Affairs*, Spring (11), pp. 103–124.

5. Lovenheim & Willem (2016).

6. Ableidinger, Joe & Hassel, Brian (2010) "Free to lead: Autonomy in highly successful charter schools," National Alliance for Public Charter Schools, Issue Brief, http://www.publiccharters.org/wp-content/uploads/2014/01/Issue_Autonomy_V4.pdf_20110330T165724.pdf.

7. Candal (2009) "Putting Children First."

8. Massachusetts Department of Elementary and Secondary Education (2010) "Massachusetts Charter School Performance Criteria v. 3.4," p. 2.

9. ibid.

10. See: Massachusetts Department of Elementary and Secondary Education, "school and district profiles" for an example of the data that DESE publishes annually: http://profiles.doe.mass.edu.

11. Allen, Jeanne, Candal, Cara & Eden, Max (2017) "Charting a new course: The case for freedom, flexibility, and opportunity through charter schools," Center for Education Reform, https://www.edreform.com/wp-content/uploads/2017/06/Charting-a-New-Course.pdf.

12. Popham, James (1999) "Why standardized tests don't measure educational quality," *Educational Leadership*, 56(6), pp. 8–15.

13. Toppo, Greg (2017) "Charter schools' thorny problem: Few students go on to earn college degrees," *USA Today*, https://www.usatoday.com/story/news/2017/03/14/charter-schools-college-degrees/99125468/.

14. O'Neill, P.T. (2009) "Multiple charter authorizing options," National Association of Charter School Authorizers, http://www.qualitycharters.org/wp-content/uploads/2015/11/PolicyGuide_MultipleCharterAuthorizingOptions_2009.07.pdf.

15. Gustafson, Joey (2013).

16. "Charter authorizers: The truth about state commissions" (2013) The Center for Education Reform, https://www.edreform.com/wp-content/uploads/2013/04/Charter-School-Authorizers-Truth-About-State-Commissions-May2013.pdf.

17. See Candal (2014) "Innovation Interrupted."

18. ibid.

19. Candal (2009) "Putting Children First."

20. Candal (2014) "Innovation Interrupted."

21. "Facilities funding for charter public schools," National Alliance for Charter Public Schools, http://www.publiccharters.org/publications/facilities-funding-for-charter-schools-2016/.

22. See chapter 5 of this book for an in-depth discussion.

23. See: McShane, Michael & Hatfield, Jen (2015) "Measuring diversity in charter school offerings," *American Enterprise Institute.*

24. Whitmire, Richard (2016) "Boston's A team of charter school leaders," *Commonwealth Magazine,* https://commonwealthmagazine.org/education/bostons-a-team-of-charter-school-leaders/.

25. That lawsuit was appealed but, in 2018, the Supreme Judicial Court dealt charter advocates another blow when it agreed with the lower court's dismissal, finding that the charter school cap does not violate the Constitution. See: Anderson, Travis, "Mass high court rejects challenge to cap on number of charter schools in the state," *The Boston Globe,* April 24, 2018.